1

RELIGION AND PSYCHOLOGY

RELIGION AND PSYCHOLOGY

E.F. O'DOHERTY

ALBA · HOUSE   NEW · YORK

SOCIETY OF ST. PAUL, 2187 VICTORY BLVD., STATEN ISLAND, NEW YORK 10314

200.19

Library of Congress Cataloging in Publication Data

O'Doherty, Eamonn Feichin.
    Religion and psychology.

    Bibliography: p.
    1. Christianity--Psychology. 2. Psychology,
Religious. I. Title.
BR110.023   200'.1'9   77-18504
ISBN 0-8189-0363-5

Nihil Obstat:
Jerome Curtin
Censor Librorum

Imprimi Potest:
✠ Dermot Ryan
Archbishop of Dublin
July 7, 1977

*The Nihil Obstat and Imprimatur
are a declaration that a book or pamphlet is considered
to be free from doctrinal or moral error. It is not implied
that those who have granted the Nihil Obstat and
Imprimatur agree with the contents,
opinions or statements expressed.*

Produced in the United States of
America by the Fathers and Brothers of the
Society of St. Paul, 2187 Victory Boulevard,
Staten Island, New York, 10314, as part of their
communications apostolate.

1 2 3 4 5 6 7 8 9 (*Current Printing: first digit*).

PREFACE

Is there a need, is there even room for still another book on religion and psychology? Recent years have seen a great increase in the number of studies broadly grouped together under "the psychology of religion." Some of these studies are more properly called studies of religious behaviour. Some have been carried out by thoroughly convinced believers in the Christian faith, others by unbelievers. Yet other studies have been concerned with using psychological and psychoanalytic insights in order to try to understand the meaning of some Christian beliefs, symbols and practices. The present volume is not a replication of these studies. Rather it is intended to fill what might be regarded as a gap in the literature. It is neither religious psychology nor the psychology of religion or of religious behaviour. It might be described as the bringing together of some theological, philosophical and psychological perspectives on a few selected human problems.

Recent years have seen many developments in theology and a remarkable growth of interest in so-called preternatural and mystical phenomena. One notes also a certain confusion in many peoples' minds about the relations between nature and grace, between the functions of religion and the nature of psychotherapy and in general between the realms of experience and the realm of faith.

This small volume, grounded in the faith, and written frankly from the standpoint of a believer who is also a psychologist, is intended to throw some light on these problems.

Individual sections and whole chapters were written at different times and some of the material has already appeared elsewhere. It is in response to what seems to be a growing demand that one feels justified in putting all the material together in one volume.

E.F.O'D.
August 1977.

Contents

RELIGION AND PSYCHOLOGY

CHAPTER I.

FREUD AND JUNG

1. Freud and Religion

Freud was an unbeliever from an early age. He refers to himself in the *Future of an Illusion* as "an infidel Jew," apparently intending the reader to understand that he had abandoned belief in any religion. We know that already while working under Brücke in 1876 he had adopted a materialistic view of man. The spirit of Brücke's institute was that psychology was the study of the nervous system and that psychical energy was nothing more than physical energy supplied by the brain cells. This was intended to be an alternative to the then rampant concept of vitalism. Vitalism as popularly understood is both philosophically and biologically faulty, representing as it does the tradition of Plato and Descartes. This concept divides man into two beings: a non-living structure composed of elementary particles in violent motion called the "body," to which is attached something else called mind or soul or psyche. These two beings simply co-exist and interact temporarily. This was foreign to Freud's thinking about man. All through the rest of his life Freud clung to the idea that he was dealing with the living organism and its processes. He used a mechanistic physical engineering model and he thought only in terms of physical energy, although he retained the terminology of the psyche and of psychical energy.

To trace some of the influences which contributed to Freud's thinking about man and religion is interesting. He had studied under Brentano during two years, 1874-76. During this time he took six courses in philosophy. Significantly, Brentano was a priest who had left the Catholic Church. He was a trained scholastic philosopher who founded modern empirical psychology, and who emphasized in his teaching the notion of process or act rather than the notion of content which psychologists had been stressing up to that point. Freud's link with Brentano was very close. It was Brentano who recommended Freud to Theodor Gomperz as the translator of part of the works of John Stuart Mill into German (cf. Merlan, 1945, 1949). Mill has been aptly named "the saint of rationalism." When the extreme rationalism of Mill is added to the thinking of Brentano about the psychophysical composite (Brentano knew St. Thomas very well), it is possible to see how Freud's thinking began to develop. From Brentano, presumably, Freud learned a great deal about the unconscious, although Brentano abandoned the term later on. From Mill he learned a great deal about the pleasure-principle because Mill's father, a pupil of Jeremy Bentham, was one of the architects of a thoroughgoing hedonism. And hedonism concentrates all human activity in the search for pleasure. As early as his twentieth year Mill had found himself constrained to go beyond the narrow hedonism of his father, just as Freud after twenty years in analytic studies found himself constrained to go "beyond the pleasure principle." Human life could not be explained by a simple maximizing of pleasure.

To these three streams of influence, Brücke's material-

ism, Brentano's psychophysical composite, and Mill's hedonism, can be added some other sources of Freud's thinking. These were: Rousseau's "social contract" theory of
civilization and culture; Darwin's view of man's descent
as an evolutionary phylogenetic process paralleled by
the ontogenetic development of the individual; and
Hobbes' view of the condition of man in nature as *bel-
lum omnium contra omnes.*" Freud thought in terms of
these different concepts and contradictory points of view.
They are the ideas which lie behind his theories in psychology and religion. He thought that if we were left to ourselves we would revert to a Hobbesian state of nature.
Thus we read:

> How ungrateful, how short-sighted after all, to strive
> for the abolition of civilization! What would then
> remain would be a state of nature that would be far
> harder to bear.

(He meant a Hobbes state of nature, not a Rousseau
state of nature.)

> It is precisely because of these dangers with which na-
> ture threatens us that we came together and created
> civilization . . . the principal task of civilization, its
> actual raison d'être is to defend us against nature.
> (Freud, 1962, p. 11.)

Freud thought of religion as part of that civilizing
process, so it was purely utilitarian and hedonistic. He
thought that religion must be evaluated, not in terms of
its being true or false, but in terms of whether or not
it is conducive to the furtherance of man's happiness.
In other words, *religion is an instrument for temporal
well-being.* This is an erroneous but not uncommon con-

cept of religion. If one accepts that religious usefulness or otherwise is a valid category, then a great deal of what Freud said is very sound. He appears to have regarded this as the only category of evaluation, but never the less the truth-falsity dimension continued to concern him.

> To assess the truth-value of religious doctrines does not lie within the scope of the present enquiry (Freud, 1928, p. 29).

He regarded religion as a neurosis because for him it was a regression to an infantile state. He also conceded that the believer has a right to go on believing. This is strange because no psychiatrist defends the maintenance of a neurosis. A certain ambivalence is apparent right through in Freud's whole approach to religious belief.

> "I still maintain," he said "that what I have written is quite harmless in one respect. No believer would let himself be led astray from his faith by these or similar arguments." (Freud 1928, p. 43.)

Earlier he had said:

> Nothing that I have said here against the true value of religion needed the support of psychoanalysis. It had been said by others long before analysis came into existence. If the application of the psychoanalytic method makes it possible to find a new argument against the truths of religion, *tant pis* for religion.

He went on:

> But, defenders of religion will by the same right make use of psychoanalysis in order to give full value to the affective significance of religious doctrines.

It is interesting to note that this is precisely what has begun to happen. So, for instance, we can now understand a great deal more of the theology of the Eucharist in terms of our identification with and oral incorporation of the loved object. We can understand some of the factors involved in marriages which have been "ratified but never consummated" in terms of analytic insights. We know a great deal more about the nature of atheism because of Freud's account of the natural history of how we came to believe in God.

Freud never thought that psychoanalysis *disproves* the teachings of religion. Moreover, Freud was never as final in his rejection of religion as some of his followers were later. There is always an ambivalence in his mind as to whether God is a projected image or whether there really is another order of reality. Thus, while teaching that "religion is an illusion," he was careful to point out that:

> an illusion is not the same thing as an error; nor is it necessarily an error . . . illusions need not necessarily be false, that is to say, unrealizable or in contradiction to reality. (Freud 1928, p. 26-7.)

In fact, according to Freud, what constitutes a particular belief an "illusion" is not its content true or false but its motivation:

> . . . we call a belief an illusion when a wish-fulfillment is a prominent factor in its motivation, and in doing so we disregard its relations to reality, just as the illusion itself sets no store by verification. (p. 27.)

He is therefore clearly saying that the truth or otherwise of a religious belief is not established by psychological statements about its origin.

Religion originates, according to Freud, in man's help-lessness before his own instinctive fears within (fear of his own aggression and the force of libido), and the threatening forces of nature without. It belongs to an early stage of human development before the child learns to handle his own internal fears and impulses and the forces of nature outside him. The affective states gener-ated by fears that well up within or are provoked from without, are coped with by the introduction of counter-affects, that is, we produce another set of emotions to cope with our fears instead of coping with them ration-ally. The function of these counter-affects is to suppress and control the fear-producing elements with which the individual finds he cannot cope rationally.

It is at this stage that the "illusion" develops. A child, when he experiences danger or uncontrollable fears, runs to his father as a source of reassurance, strength and com-fort. The father is also a source of authority, reward and punishment. The child discovers that he can win affection by obeying the commands of his parents. And above all, he has the guilt of the oedipal phase of development to cope with. The violation of the parricide and incest taboos demands expiation. (Freud assumed that morals were not essentially different from taboos; they were, according to his thinking, merely the expressions of taboos in de-veloped societies). What is appropriate to the child at that level of development is "natural" for the child. Freud thinks that the adult tries the same childish mechanism, runs for comfort to the father, but the father is no longer there. The adult therefore projects the image of the fa-ther and generates a counter-affect. He calls the image God and the counter-affect the love of God or reward for good deeds and such like. But while this is good and natural for the child, it is a regression for the adult, therefore it is neurotic. This is the substance of *The Future of an Illusion*. The illusion is the reification of the projected father-image.

"Religion" derives therefore from the fact that the adult who cannot cope rationally with his problems "regresses" to the level of infantile defence; religion is a reinstatement of infantile behavior patterns, but with the important difference that because these infantile behavior patterns are inappropriate at adult levels they now constitute a neurosis. This is why, according to Freud, "religion . . . (is) . . . thus . . . the universal obsessional neurosis of humanity." (Freud, 1928, p. 39.)

Underlying this theory of Freud's is the fallacy of *psychomechanistic parallelism*. This is the fallacy of assuming that because two behavior-patterns are observed to exhibit the same constituents or are reducible to the same component elements, they are to be attributed to the same psychological mechanism. In spite of the fact that Freud was aware of the invalidity of this kind of reasoning, as Fromm (1950) points out, he falls into the trap. He observes the parallels between infantile, neurotic and religious behavior: the behavior of the child, its babbling and its efforts to placate its father are paralleled by the compulsive behavior of the neurotic trying to allay guilt, and these are both in Freud's opinion identical with the ritual religious behavior of placating the deity and allaying guilt. Freud says therefore that religion is a regression to infantile or neurotic behavior.

Since, for Freud, moral injunctions and prohibitions were essentially the same as primitive taboos and were of purely utilitarian value (ministering to our personal comfort or preserving order in society), the notions of an objective moral order and real guilt were wholly foreign to his thought. He therefore, together with many psy-

chologists and psychoanalysts, uses the word "guilt" always with the connotation "emotional" (and therefore
neurotic) attached to it. Religion thus becomes a means
of getting rid of neurotic guilt, on the one hand by placating "god," the projected father image, and on the
other hand by ritual cleansing of the guilt incurred in
the violation of taboo.

Much of what Freud says about the genesis of religion
corresponds to the theologian's traditional teaching about
the *debased* form of religion called superstition and does
in fact account for some forms of "primitive" religion.
Freud always uses the word "primitive" in a consistent
sense to refer to undeveloped or underdeveloped states
of society where conceptual thinking is at a minimum.
In the nineteenth century, from studies of comparative
religion, it was thought that the evolution of religion
was from primitive animism through polytheism to monotheism. Freud believed this. Frazer's *Golden Bough*
(1922) described the evolution of religious thought from
primitive animistic belief in spirits dwelling in trees,
streams, etc., through the idea of several gods, to a belief
in one God. It is now known, however, that the polytheism and animism are degenerate forms: man begins
with a belief in God but monotheism may degenerate
over time to polytheism and animism.

In studying superstition one finds emerging the emotional dependencies, the magic rituals, the taboos, all of
which Freud saw in what he observed of religion. It is
worth remembering that what Freud observed of religion
was its manifestation in *sick* people. Freud was concerned
with taboo mechanisms in sick and disturbed people rather
than with moral behavior. He had eliminated in advance
the possibility of an intellect having a function of its own.
In Freud's thinking the processes of the organism are the

only reality of man. If we consider only the irrational, the subrational and the prerational functions (or, to generalize these, the sensory functions), then we see that what Freud says is largely true but incomplete. It prescinds from the intellect and the will.

Idea and Image. The *idea* of God must be distinguished from the *image* of God. Empirical psychologists from Locke onwards tend to use the word "idea" to mean "image." An image is sensory in character: a dog can form an image of a bone, an infant can form an image; a child or an adult can form an image of God as an old man in the sky with a long beard. But an image is not an idea. An idea is a concept and concepts are products of the intellect. The concept of God is what we express to ourselves of the nature of God: infinite being, three persons. The fatherhood of God is a concept. An image of God as a man with a beard is in no sense the same thing as the idea of God. Graven images were prohibited in the Old Testament because the graven image would not represent the *concept* of God and there was an ever-present danger that the people would lapse into idolatry. The primitive mind could regress before the concept was firmly fixed. For Locke and the Empiricists, if one accounts for the image of God one has then accounted for the idea of God, since they do not distinguish between these two. Freud also failed to make this distinction.

The fact that we project an image of God does not mean that the image is wrong or that the idea of God is illusory. We have to express our idea of God somehow and we cannot do so in any way that is adequate to the reality. The reality is infinite so we express our idea in negative ways and by analogy. The *idea* of God is of omnipotent, omniscient Being, uncaused cause, but these are difficult ideas. We tend, therefore, to make use of imagery to bear the not wholly formed ideas derived from metaphysics and theology.

As well as the distinction between image and idea, a distinction must be made between the affective and cognitive dimensions of the image of the deity. To some even still the image of God in the Old Testament is sometimes seen in the affective dimension as that of a God to be feared: Vengeance is mine saith the Lord.

In the New Testament it is the same God but the affective aspect is changed: "When you pray, say 'Our Father'." 'Father' here is a projection of the human notion of paternity. The emotional attitude of the child to his father is carried over into the idea of God. In different cultures we can see differences in the emotional loading of the image. In some societies the family constellation is patriarchal. The father is the source of strength, rules, authority. The child's attitude to the father in these societies will be one of fear, reverence, dread, but perhaps very little love. In present-day Western cultures love is dominant but the element of fear may also be present.

When the child begins to form an image of God he usually bases it on the already introjected image of his father. The child's *idea* of God grows from the projected father-image with all its affective tones of fear or love. The relationship the child has had with his father can color the affective tone of the idea he forms of God. If the father-figure is extremely punitive this will be carried through even in the idea. The individual may assent intellectually to the conceptual idea of merciful God, Redeemer, etc. but some of the original affective tone will remain. Freud's insights have enabled us to understand phenomena like atheism in ways that were not possible before his time.

Freud thought that because he had discovered the

genesis of the *image* of God he had therefore accounted
for the *idea* of God and thus explained away the existence of God. He also thought that because the affective
dimension of the image could be explained this also accounted for the idea. Freud's thinking was colored by
his rejection of his own father and of his Jewish religion,
and moreover it is important to note that he was an
atheist before he began his studies on psychoanalysis. It is
sometimes thought that Freud studied the child's development, discovered the genesis of the image of God and
therefore rejected religion, but this is not so. To give an
account of how a person forms any idea is in no sense
to account for the validity of the idea. Accounting for
the formation of an idea does not account for the content of the idea. Freud did not account for the content,
nor indeed wholly for the image. He does account for
one dimension of how we form the image of God and
gives some insight into the emotional aspects of the image.

The problem of the existence of God is not a problem in or for psychology, nor is it a problem in or for
cultural anthropology. The problem of the existence of
anything is very different from the problem of how we
came to form the concept or to project the image. The
image we have of the unicorn is very different from the
question of whether or not the unicorn exists. The fallacy
of historicism is the fallacy of confusing the history of
the origin of something with the validity of the item
itself whose history is being studied. The history of ideas
is a valid study but it is not to be identified with the
study of speculative philosophy. Freud said that he had
accounted for the history of the idea of God but in fact
what he had done was to account for part of the history
of the image of God. The Bishop of Woolwich in *Honest
to God* (1963) was trying to get rid of the projected

image of God but he confused the image with the idea and ended up with pantheism.

A further dimension of the introjected father-image is the concept of guilt. In Freud the notion of guilt is intrinsically bound up with the image of God. For Freud and his followers, as for many legal thinkers today, the notion of "guilt" is almost always synonymous with *neurotic* guilt, that is, an unhealthy state of the emotions. Freud says that the adult experiences neurotic guilt as a result of violation of the taboos or mores of his social group. He seeks relief for the guilt he has incurred by ritual expiation. Freud equates the ritual expiation of guilt and taboo with what in religion would be called prayer and sacrifice. Freud's equation is legitimate as far as neurotic guilt is concerned, but this is not at all the same thing as an act of worship or prayer or expiation for moral transgression, although Freud thinks it is. He says that the child's guilt is allayed by the parent-figure. He thinks that the adult is in the same state as the child in a violation of taboo and that he regresses to an infantile level in seeking to expiate his guilt by ritual processes of religion.

The mistake of Freud and some of his followers was to think that all guilt was neurotic guilt or at least that all emotional guilt was neurotic. Emotional guilt is not neurotic. It can be healthy and its total absence in an individual may be a pathological process, as in the psychopath who experiences no sense of compunction for his anti-social acts.

Since all guilt is neurotic according to Freud, all religion in his view is a way of getting rid of guilt by placating the gods and undergoing ritual cleansing from the violation of taboo. Freud's theory is that we generate our own god by projection of the father-image. We need this god because our own father has failed us, and as we grow up we try to get rid of anxiety by falling back on religion. While this is not an account of religion, it does give some understanding of some people's misuse of religion.

2. *Jung and Religion*

Jung had already broken with Freud on the question of sexuality and its role in infancy and the neuroses. He soon took up the question of religion and was seen by many as teaching a more acceptable doctrine than Freud. In Freud's view religion was an illusion, it was the great mass neurosis of mankind. Jung said that far from religion being a neurosis, he had never, he claimed, had a patient whose neurosis was not due to his lack of religion, nor had he ever cured a patient whose cure was not due to his return to religion. The origin of neurosis lay precisely in the absence of religion. The formula was attractive and was accepted by many who thought that Jung was using the words *neurosis* and *religion* in their ordinary public meaning. It took a long time to realize that Jung was not using the word *neurosis* in any strictly medical sense, and that by *religion* he meant a purely psychological phenomenon composed of emotional and imaginative elements, from which all rational, spiritual, supernatural and objective content was expunged. To be quite fair to Jung, he claimed that he simply prescinded from all such content, of which he knew nothing. He thought that such things were in any case unknowable. He prescinded from the existence of God and regarded the propositions of all religions as equally true, having what he called "psychological truth," that is, they were true for those who believed them. There is no objectivity in Jungian ideas because what is true for each individual is the truth. By religion he meant a dynamism of the unconscious, essentially irrational in kind, which served as a unifying function or value-system around which or upon which one might build a consistent life-pattern.

A good deal of the language of Jung reads as if it were a defence of religion and of its importance in mental health, as against the Freudian contention that religion itself is a neurosis, an illusion, which with more and better analysis will pass away. Beginning with materialism and atheism, it was inevitable that Freud would deny all objectivity to religion. But the advantage of this is that the reader knows where he stands with Freud. It is otherwise with Jung. He constantly reiterates his contention that he is an empirical psychologist, observing and recording what he sees. But he is more than this in fact; he is basically a Kantian philosopher and an agnostic. It is possible also that he is an atheist, since "god" is a projection of an unconscious fantasy; the differences between "gods" are constituted apparently by their efficacy in integrating different parts of the psyche.

Jung holds that all religions are schools of psychotherapy, all have the same goal, all treat and heal the suffering of the soul and the suffering of the body caused by the soul. Suffering of soul, according to Jung, is a natural illness, since he does not believe in grace or in the supernatural. He talks of the "great psychotherapeutic systems we call religions." (Jung 1954, p. 193). "Religion . . . a system of psychic healing" (ibid., p. 121). The idea of God originates (as it did for Freud) in projecting unconscious elements on to an object which is thought to exist in a special way, and statements about God are in reality statements about the unconscious element which is projected. "Religious projection offers a much more effectual help" (for solving conflicts). "In this one keeps the conflict in sight" (care, pain, anxiety and so on), "and gives it over to a personality standing outside oneself, the Divinity." Some theologians seem to have accepted Jung's point of view that religion is a form of psychotherapy (cf. Goldbrunner, 1955 and 1958). But further research and better psychology and theology have led to a clearer understanding of Jung's position. Cox (1959) points out that psychotherapy is not an alternative to Christianity. Jungian analysis, leading to individuation (Jung's concept of the process whereby we become the sort of person we ought to be) is not a substitute for justification. Religion is not essentially irrational and the soul is really distinct from its functions. For Jung, soul and psyche were regarded as one and the same. White (1960) taught that soul and psyche were in fact identical, but this is quite clearly erroneous. There is a real distinction between the soul and its faculties.

Psychoanalysis is concerned with the psyche (the apparatus of processes of the psychophysical composite), while religion is concerned with the spiritual welfare of the whole man but specifically with the soul in whose essence grace resides.

Many psychotherapists and some psychoanalysts have tended to think that their task was to produce the "ideal man," the "good man," and that this could be better done by psychoanalysis than by the grace of God. It seems quite certain that this is the fundamental error of Jung, whose "therapy" is a form of *re*education, *re*formation of the personality, to produce a sort of Stoic-Confucian-Kantian-Humanist-Jungian-Christian. It is doubtful if therapy is the right word. The process seems to be not so much the curing of an ill as a rebirth.

3. *Religion and scientific thinking*

Every new break-through in the area of human thought or experience has been turned into a conflict with religion. When Peter Abelard tried to use dialectic in the twelfth century he was condemned by the Council of Soissons. Hugh of St. Victor left the University of Paris on the ground that any sort of knowledge was a threat to religion. Down through the centuries the same controversies arise over and over again. William of Ockham, the humanism of the fifteenth century, the rise of science, the new philosophy originating in Descartes, the new logic deriving from Bacon, the theories of Darwin, all have been the occasion of a major conflict with the Church. The same holds for psychology.

This problem is a reciprocal one. Some who are competent in psychology find themselves constrained to reject religion and some religious persons regard psychology as a threat. The difficulty here is inherent in human nature itself, not in either religion or psychology as such. Theologians are the inevitable product of their own cultural milieu and their thinking is conditioned by the socially determined attitudes of their own time. In a cultural context where the intervention of the preternatural in natural affairs was taken for granted, it was inevitable that some purely psychological phenomena would be regarded as "religious" manifestations. It is very difficult to eradicate from the mind of man vestiges of primitive ways of thinking. It is equally wrong, however, to swing to the rational to the exclusion of any other explanation and dismiss all religion as superstition.

There could be no conflict in principle between revelation on the one hand and the psychologist's picture of the psyche on the other. If our understanding of mind and psyche bears any relation to reality, then we shall find that revelation, if it took place, will have been made in terms of the psyche that we know. The fact that we discover that religion is in terms of the psyche as the psychologist discovers it to be, does not mean that religion is therefore not true. We have only one psyche and the fact that the same processes operate in the learning of religion as in other areas does not falsify either the one or the other. The assumption and arguments of the analysts appear to be that if it could be shown that religion is related to man's needs and that it takes account of both his rational and subrational processes, then it must be naturalistic in its origin. The corollary of this seems to be that if there were such a thing as true religion, it would have to be wholly unrelated to the human psyche.

The facts that the idea of God is borne in human images or that prayer is akin to ritual, appear to have constrained the analysts to say that therefore religion is a subrational process. On the contrary, however, since religion is God's revelation to man we should expect to find in it just those elements that cater to our needs. If God reveals himself to man he will do so in terms of man's nature and through the normal channels of acquiring knowledge. The fact that a religious function satisfies a non-rational process or need does not negate its religious value. But we must be clear that the religious value does not derive from the infrarational.

Jung's concept of religion is that it is a set of values deriving precisely from the infrarational. By infrarational in Jung's terminology is meant the shadow, the *anima*, the unconscious, and all the other typical Jungian concepts. Concepts like archetypes and mandalas were introduced by Jung. We do use many symbols in religion and there is often no way other than symbol to express certain religious concepts. A symbol is a sensory presentation, one of whose functions is to convey the "ineffable." If we are inarticulate about something we can only express it in symbol. Symbol can also, however, be a shorthand expression of things about which we could be very articulate, but Jung does not advert to this.

We need symbols because we are creatures of sense and intellect. The dependence, interdependence and inseparability of sense and intellect necessitate the use of symbols at once sensory and intellectual. If the symbol has in fact no intellectual content, then it is not a function of religion but of magic. The signs of the Zodiac were intended to be symbols with intellectual content. They lost this with the development of science and are now relegated to the area of "magic." The Star of David is a sensory symbol with enormous intellectual content. So also are the symbols of incense, candles, the cross. If we respond to symbols only as sensory, then we are functioning at the sensory level. The child does this sometimes because there is a good deal of "magical" thinking at the preoperational levels of intellectual development. If this primitive "magical" element persists at adult levels, it debases religion. Sprinkling holy water, which is a genuine religious ritual, may degenerate to the level of magic if, for example, one feels compelled to sprinkle a specified number of times in order that it be efficacious in some particular way. Statues sometimes have magical thinking associated with them. The Greek iconoclasts, the Cromwellians and some of the Reformers had an inkling of what could happen if the sensory elements in religious behavior were allowed to predominate, and the danger of substituting magical thinking for religion.

4. *Soul, Psyche and Mind*

One problem that has to be faced in the area of religion and mental health is that of attempting to define the terms *soul*, *psyche* and *mind*. It is very important that these three be distinguished one from another, especially in view of the enormous influence of Jungian thinking on some theologians and psychologists. The Jungian idea appears to be that there is no real distinction, but only a notional one, between the terms soul and psyche. It is true that soul and psyche were at one time synonyms, the one being used as a translation of the other. But the real problem is this: when the psychologist uses the term psyche, is he talking about something which is only logically or notionally distinct from soul, or is there in fact a real distinction between them? This is not simply a theoretical problem for philosophers. It has become customary among an influential group of psychologists to assert that "holiness is wholeness," to assume with Jung that only the religious man can be mentally healthy, that neurosis is due to the absence of religion. This is based on a Humean point of view according to which the mind *is* its own processes. It has been contended (White, 1960) that the welfare of soul and psyche are one. This is predicated on the proposition that soul and psyche are identical.

Soul refers to the substantial, spiritual, indivisible, indestructible life-principle which, when united with the material principle, constitutes the human being. The human soul is capable of an existence independent of matter, with functions which are not necessarily or intrinsically bound up with matter. Never the less the soul is what makes a living organism to be a living organism. Soul is not restricted to the human species. Every living organism, even at plant level, has a soul or life-principle. In the case of man, soul happens to be a spirit. Spirit is the mode of existence of substances which are independent of the limitations of space and time. Soul in man is the spiritual principle, the element in our composition which in itself is free from the laws of space and time, but which *by virtue of its present existence* is bound in the space-time continuum. The joint result of the fusion of soul and body is the living organism or the psychophysical composite. There is a tendency sometimes to think of soul as a spirit dwelling in or hovering around an organism. This idea of an organism with its own functions to which a soul is, so to speak, "attached" is a Cartesian concept. We must think of the living organism, not just as a linking of soul to body, but as a fusion resulting in one being, that is, the psychophysical composite. Whatever is predicated of the person as person is predicated of the living organism. The problem for philosophy and psychology is not *How can body and soul be united*? The tendency of philosophers since the time of Plato has been to think in these terms. The real problem, however, is *How can body and soul be separated*? The soul is a co-constituent principle of the living organism, not something added to it. There is only one being with two co-constituent principles. Soul is the name of a co-principle of being whose function it is to be the source of the processes which empirically differentiate living matter from non-living matter.

The term *psyche* refers to the amalgam of all the functions of the organism in its organic existence. It is the amalgam or structure of all the processes which have their roots in the soul, and in addition, all the content that the mind has acquired throughout the years of our existence in this world. The functions of the organism

derive from the soul as co-principle of being. The soul is
the first principle or ultimate source of the functions
of the living organism: metabolic functions, functions
of nutrition and growth, generative functions, functions
of local motion, sensation, emotion, intelligence are all
functions of the soul, or more accurately, the complex of
all these functions *is* the psyche. The psyche is not something which "has" these functions; it is not something
to which these functions occur; the psyche is the set of
these functions. Psyche is a collective noun and refers
to this amalgam of functions. All the functions of the
living organism derive from the soul, but the soul is not
its own functions.

Only in God are function and source of function identical. So in the human person the functions of the soul
(in other words, the psyche) are distinct from soul as
the source of the functions. The psyche as distinct from
the soul is psycho-physical. The soul is spiritual, free
from the laws of space and time, but the psyche is bound
to the living organism since it is the set of functions of
the living organism. It is the way in which the living
organism functions. If we think of the anatomy of the
organism and then think of the physiology of the organism, we have a rather poor analogy of the relations of
soul and psyche.

Mind refers to certain processes within the psyche
which usually bear the predicate *mental*. All processes of
the living organism are processes of the psyche but not
all can be described as mental processes; for example,
cellular fission, metabolism, nutrition, reproductive processes. When we come to consider actual and positive
experience we are coming into the area of the mental.
In locomotion, for example, there can be a conscious experience, but motion itself is not mental. We call certain

functions *mental* because they are the kinds of functions that could occur consciously although they do not necessarily occur consciously. Unconscious wishes and desires are still mental. Up to the end of the nineteenth century the word *mental* would have been limited on the whole to conscious processes, whereas now conscious, unconscious, cognitive and conative activities are all included under the words *mental* or *mind*. The psyche, however, is far more extensive than the mind. It embraces all the functions of the living organism including the functions of intellect and will.

The person as living organism carries out the following activities:

(a) Chromosomal, genetic, cellular processes. These are activities of the subject as person.

(b) Nutritive, generative and metabolic functions. Again, these are activities of the subject as person. They do not simply "happen."

(c) Local motion processes: the living organism walks out the door. We must avoid any Cartesian tendency to think that the *soul* or person pilots a *body* through the door.

(d) Sensory processes: internal and external senses, emotions, instincts. It is the whole person who feels afraid. It is not a conscious *soul* or *mind* which happens to be a living organism which feels fear.

(e) Intellectual and volitional processes. These two are not functions of living matter as such, they are functions of the person who is the living organism, that is, they are functions of the two co-principles which form the living organism.

All the above processes are operations of the organism in its organic existence. There are other areas where the organism undergoes experiences not as organism but as matter, for example, organisms are subject to the law of gravity.

The psyche (the functioning of the organism) derives from the soul as first principle. The term *mind* is restricted to some of these functions. Mind is not a part of the soul but is the name of the group of functions listed above as *mental*. The specifically *human* functions which come under the head of mental are those of intellect and will. Intellect and will (i.e. knowledge and goal seeking) are functions of the soul as spirit, but all other organic processes are functions of the fusion of soul and body, that is, they are functions of living matter. Everything which is *psychical* is also organic because the psyche is the functioning of the organism. The only things which are not *physiologically based* are the processes of intellect and will because they are not the result of the convergent operation of two co-principles, matter and soul. The functions of intellect and will are functions of spirit alone, not of the psychophysical composite.

Relations of soul and psyche: Since the soul is the principle of life, and since the human person is a living organism, some functions of the psyche will always be operative, otherwise the person would not be alive. The soul is a dynamic substance always in act. But because soul and psyche are not identical what is predicable of one is not necessarily predicable of the other. For example, in the case of mental deficiency what is in question is a deficiency of the psyche, not a deficiency of the soul. The soul of a mentally defective child is complete in its own species and this is easier to understand if we remember that the soul of a mentally defective infant will be able to enjoy the vision of God for all eternity. In the same way, the illnesses which are known as the neuroses and the psychoses are disorders of the psyche. It is the *person* who is ill, not the soul. When we talk about "sickness of the soul" or "the soul dead in sin," we are talking in metaphor. But one must always beware of the danger of taking metaphor literally. The soul is not literally dead because this is a metaphysical impossibility given that the soul is immortal. "Sickness" or "death" of the *soul* refer to our analogical participation in the divine life, the life of grace, which is a very different matter. When one talks about a psyche which is sick, however, one is speaking literally and not in metaphor. The soul "sick" with sin (i.e. "sick" in a theological sense) is quite capable of a mental life free from natural illness, and conversely a soul may be free from sin, but the psyche very sick indeed. If soul and psyche are identical, as some writers have contended, whatever is true of one is true of the other so that welfare of soul and welfare of psyche become one and the same thing. In the same way, a disorder of psyche becomes a disorder of the soul. It is often said, though. it is in fact not true, that spiritual wellbeing is proportioned to, or even intrinsically dependent on, or at any rate related to, mental health; and conversely, that mental illness is related to loss of spiritual well being. This is a confusion which it is difficult to eradicate, perhaps because it seems obvious and even attractive. In Victor White's book *Soul and Psyche* we have an illustration of the lexicoprapher's fallacy (i.e. words must mean what the lexicographer says they mean). So if psyche meant soul (anima) in Aristotle's day, then *psychology* must be the science of the soul. According to White, the wellbeing of the psyche and wellbeing of the soul are the same thing. It follows that if the wellbeing of the psyche is the prerogative of psychotherapy then psychotherapy must be good for the soul, and conversely it seems to follow from the logic of this that the practice of religion is the panacea for mental illness. Keenan (1950) makes a similar and even more fundamental mistake in terminology: he takes the line that the minister of religion has a *cure* of souls, which must also mean that he cures sickness of soul. This is a faulty translation from the Latin where *cura* means care of souls rather than "cure of souls."

Mental illness and wrong doing are quite distinct concepts. Wrong doing reflects on the *anima* or soul. According to White, a disorder of soul automatically becomes a disorder of psyche. If he were right it would follow that the more and the greater one's sins the less they would be sins, because the greater the psychological disorder the more responsibility is diminished. Certain concepts of Buddhism, Mohammedanism and other religions show the same confusion between soul and psyche. They take the notion of the morally good man and speak of him in terms of health of soul. The Buddhist notion of purification corresponds very closely to the notion of moral responsibility. The confusion between the morally good man and the mentally healthy man manifests itself in many different forms. The good man is an ethical ideal, and because we use the word healthy in a metaphorical or analogical sense, we are then tempted to equate the ethical concept of the good man with the natural concept of the healthy man. Health of mind is confused with moral wellbeing, when, for example, a psychotherapist claims to "cure" a patient of his guilt. What he does is to relieve the patient's neurotic state but he is not necessarily improving the moral stature of the patient. An analogous error is the notion that by carrying out some form of religious ritual one will become mentally healthy. The conceptual confusion in these two areas leads to a certain confusion about roles: sometimes individuals who are suffering from a mental illness think they should consult a priest, and individuals with a moral problem think they should consult a psychiatrist.

Another example of confusion in concepts related to soul and psyche is the readiness with which we apply psychological-psychiatric categories, which if they were true would nullify the argument we wish to put forward. For example, if it were true that Hitler was a paranoiac then he would have to be exonerated from moral responsibility in World War II. To the extent that an individual is mentally ill, he must be exonerated from guilt. The stormtroopers and the guards at Auchswitz were mentally healthy, otherwise they could not be held responsible for their deeds. It is difficult for some people to accept the difference between the categories of mental health or illness and moral good or evil. It should be remembered, however, that a capacity for evil is part of the human condition, and indeed, paradoxically, a condition of mental health. The reason for the latter statement is that a human person incapable of choosing evil would be either seriously defective in intelligence or seriously psychotic.

There has been in the past and there still remains a vast confusion between the concepts of happiness, contentment, satisfaction and health, particularly in so far as these are thought to be related to religion. Happiness and health are not the same. It is true that for the normal functioning of the average man a modicum of material goods and a modicum of happiness are indispensable. But it is not the function of religion to make man happy, just as it is not the function of religion to make man healthy. Similarly, it is sometimes thought that the function of religion is to rid the individual of his anxieties, to enable him to achieve "peace of soul" in various ways. If one thinks that the function of religion is to console or to eliminate anxiety or to produce some other temporal good, then one is thinking of religion as an instrumental good. Sometimes religion may incidentally produce effects of this kind, but it is not the primary function of religion to do these things. Religion properly understood and taken seriously will indeed have as one of its effects the generation of anxiety. It is almost impossible for the mature human being to think of eternity and ultimate realities without anxiety. The "fear of the Lord" is the beginning of religion, and religion, far from being an anxiety-allaying mechanism, can actually generate anxiety. Religion is often represented to people as though its primary function were to relieve anxiety. To teach the truths of religion primarily because they are consoling or reassuring, or for any instrumental purpose, is a distortion of religion. In the very same way, people are sometimes inclined to cast religion or the minister of religion for a sort of witch doctor or magician role, and to think that it is his function or the function of religion to make them happy. It may in fact at times be necessary for the minister of religion to make people unhappy, to produce in them a need for an agonizing reappraisal, to shake their complacency, to provoke anxiety and even anger. The formal function of religion as such is the worship of God, the manifestation of his glory in time and in eternity, and by this means the sanctification and salvation of human persons. In the vision of God, man achieves happiness, but it is not the primary function of religion that man should achieve happiness either in this world or hereafter.

Mental illness and sanctity: It is held by some writers that sanctity, since it means the perfecting of the personality through grace, is incompatible with mental illness. The thinking here is that God would not perfect with supernatural grace a defective unit in the natural order. Those who hold this point of view say that God first perfects the personality in the natural order, and subsequently in the supernatural order, so that mental illness must be cured before sanctity is possible. This is the opinion of Goldbrunner (1955, 1959) and White (1955, 1960). If one identifies soul with psyche the perfecting of one is equivalent to the perfecting of the other. But the psyche is really distinct from the soul in the way in which any set of functions is really distinct from the source of those functions. It is not therefore true that the perfecting in the supernatural order is in strict linear continuity with perfecting in the natural order. During a full-blown psychosis a "human act" cannot be performed, so acts which bring about an increase of grace are not possible, except in the case of an individual who was fit and well enough to make a choice before the onset of the illness. This choice will then continue to operate throughout the illness, so that the acts of the individual will have a supernatural value.

In a neurosis the case is different. It may very well happen that the act is all the more meritorious because the person is neurotic. In the case of a neurosis the human act is made more difficult because voluntariety is impaired, but it is still a human act. In a psychosis voluntariety is suspended temporarily or permanently, partially or totally. In a neurosis the functioning of the intellect and will is impaired, but not suspended. Since it is more difficult for an individual to behave virtuously in these circumstances, the act is for that very reason more meritorious. Many holy people were in the natural order demonstrably neurotic. Sanctity and psychosis are, however, incompatible, because sanctity in the sense of what the saints achieved is the result of heroic virtue. Heroic voluntary actions are not possible to psychotics, only antecedent choices.

Culture and values: Mental health is compatible with any transculturally viable value system, but there are ways of life which are not transculturally viable. One example of this is in the group in Canada known as the Doukhobors, (cf. Woodcock and Avakumovic, 1968). The concept of "transcultural viability" excludes the Doukhobor way of life. Beatniks, hippies and groups of this kind are not "ways of life" because in order to be viable a way of life must involve descent and extension through time. There are some life-styles which are so extraordinary that it may seem that merely to belong to one of these groups is an indication of mental disturbance. One of the delusions of Western society, however, is to think that any way of life which does not conform to the life style of Western society must necessarily be mentally unhealthy. This of course does not follow. The Sikhs in India might seem to the superficial Western observer to have all the characteristics of the obsessional-compulsive, but the Sikh mode of life is quite compatible with full mental health. The "good man" too can be differently conceived in different societies, and as conceived in a given culture may not be transculturally viable, for example, a "good" Nazi. But it was quite possible to be mentally healthy and be a "good" Nazi. Mental health is compatible with a variety of errors of intellect. Believers tend sometimes to confuse the categories here and say that because an individual is an atheist he must be mentally ill. It cannot be claimed that atheists like Bertrand Russell were voluntarily, consciously rejecting a proposition they knew to be true, and there is certainly no question of mental illness in an individual of Russell's stature.

CHAPTER II

MENTAL HEALTH, RELIGION AND NEUROSIS

1. *Mental Health*

There are two distinct scales of mental health, the pathological scale and the maturational scale. The pathological scale extends from very severe psychotic conditions to the mere absence of discernible psychopathology. The second scale is the maturational scale, or the scale of positive mental health, extending from the level of simple absence of psychopathology to the full natural perfecting of the personality. At this level of full psychological maturity reason is freed from the dominance of non-rational forces as far as this is possible in our present existence, consciousness is freed from obsession with self, emotional life is controlled with due moderation, and good interpersonal relations are established. This second scale means the gradual emergence of the rational man from his pre-rational or subrational chrysalis.

The concept of mental health means a great deal more than the absence of mental illness. It connotes a degree of maturity of mind and emotional development commensurate with an individual's chronological age. It demands a high level of integration of the personality; it presupposes a judgment freed from the distortions due to emotional pressures, and it demands a degree of extraversion which yet leaves sufficient room for introversion in the form of insight leading to self-knowledge.

In general, mental illness is a pathological condition of the emotions or of the imagination, or of both emotions and imagination. It is not an illness of the soul or of the intellect but it can fetter the soul and cripple the intellect; that is to say, a mentally ill person is working against a great handicap, since to the extent to which he is ill his freedom is limited. A neurotic condition admits of all degrees of severity, from almost indiscernible mild forms of disturbance which most people experience at some time or other, to the very distinctive conditions of major hysteria or hypochondria. But mild or severe, it always involves a conflict of intra- or interpersonal relations within oneself or with other persons. This type of conflict produces any one or any combination of the following: anxiety, egoism, infantile dependence, immoderate aggressiveness, depression, feelings of despair, a sense of being "shut in," distrust of others, or a sense of being persecuted or at any rate unjustly treated and certainly misunderstood, self-depreciation, tears of self-pity, and emotional rigidity or apathy (which are often mistaken for strong-mindedness and self-control).

It is important to note that neurotic conflict is (at least to some extent) unconscious, and its effect on consciousness and therefore on behavior is involuntary. The result is that exhortation from without to more intense moral endeavour is often if not always fruitless. The pressure of the conflict on consciousness must be eased first, either by resolving the conflict entirely or at least by making its source fully conscious so that its relevance and influence are understood, and so that the individual's behavior (including his thought-processes which are for the moment governed by irrational forces) may be brought under the control of rationality. There is a sense in which this is much more a matter of fundamental education of the personality than of therapy applied to an illness.

In the first scale of mental health, the pathological scale, religion as such has no function. It is not the rôle of religion to help people up the pathological scale from mental illness to mental health. A certain confusion between the two scales of mental health leads to a good deal of misunderstanding in the realms of religion and psychology. People who are ill, either mentally or physically, sometimes regard their illness as a punishment for moral fault. This is a primitive prerational attitude. A corollary of this is the idea that more and more prayer and more frequent reception of the sacraments will cure illness. If a person is suffering from an illness, physical or mental, it is not the function of religion to cure him, nor is illness the result of lack of religion or neglect of religion. This kind of thinking is also a carry-over of primitive thought-categories. It might indeed appear that there is a certain theological basis for these ideas in the doctrine of the Fall of Man, which teaches that all illness and death itself are punishments for sin. This is true, but illness and death are not punishments for individual acts of individual human beings. They are the punishment of the human race as such.

On the second scale of mental health, the maturational scale, religion has a function to perform. The first thing to consider is the elevated state of human nature before the Fall. After the Fall this elevated human nature was reduced to what would have been its "natural" level, but with many further weakening processes involved as well. The Fall meant a double step down for human nature: man was created on the elevated plane; after the

Fall he went back, not to the state he would have been in if he had been created on the natural plane, but to an even lower state. His nature was weakened as a result of original sin. This means that grace has two functions to perform: it has to restore human nature to the supernatural state in which God created it, and it has to be an antidote to the weakening of human nature. Even with grace, however, man does not reach his former state of integrity.

The second (maturational) scale of mental health is the scale of rationality running from the amorphous, prerational personality of the infant (free, however, from pathological symptoms) up to the full perfection of the development of the adult human personality. The emergence of rationality from the prerational is the maturation process, and it is part of the function of grace to facilitate the emergence of rationality and the attainment of the highest possible level of moral behavior. If it could be seen that a population was demonstrably behaving in a moral way because of grace, this would not mean the disappearance of all weakness, but where grace is operating we should be able to expect a growth in sheer civilization, as in early Christendom and in other religions as well. It is true that many mature people have no religion and there are other ways of acquiring maturity: good will can be a vehicle of grace. But it is the function of religion as a vehicle of grace to help the maturation process.

Personality is the source of "intentional" behavior or behavior that is purposive and meaningful. There is an immediate relationship between person and behavior. One mistake of nineteenth century psychologists was to regard behavior as a product of a specific faculty. Behavior is mediated by specific faculties but it is produced by the person. At adult level behavior proceeds from conative through cognitive levels to action. In childhood this can be short-circuited and the child proceeds straight from emotion (the conative) to action. Behavior we call religious ought to involve the cognitive and the rational. It should never parallel the child's behavior which is infra-rational and proceeds from emotion or instinct to action. An action which proceeds directly from anxiety or any other emotional state to "religious" activity is a parallel at adult level of the infrarational behavior of the child.

2. *Religion and psychological Distortions*

Given religion as a factor in maturation, it should follow that the more dedicated and "religious" a person is the more mature he should be. This is not always the case, however, because some individuals instead of allowing themselves to respond to maturing experiences, hide behind so-called "religious" activity, and use religion as a problem-solving device, as a defense mechanism or in some other neurotic fashion. There is little doubt that some people at times use religion as a way of refusing to cope rationally with reality. An obvious case is the Christian Scientist's attitude to medical aid. Many adults are at times guilty in the name of religion of escaping from reality in analogous ways. We should of course turn to God in all our difficulties, but if we turn away from the difficulty simply because it is a difficulty, and pray because it is easier to pray than to tackle the problem realistically, then we are using religion as a problem-solving device.

There are other ways in which people import into religion, or at any rate into their attitude towards it, elements which savor of unhealthy thinking or even of psychopathology. The compulsive-obsessional states, for example, are characterized by repetitive ritualistic patterns of behavior, easily identifiable when the condition is very marked. When the condition is less marked one does not notice the compulsive element, and very often it is difficult to distinguish between this compulsive element and the simple formation of habits. A habit is a facilitating mechansim which for good or ill makes the carrying out of an action easier and sometimes almost automatic. But in the compulsive condition emotion predominates, usually emotional guilt or "guilt-feelings," and it is this which determines the subsequent behavior. Thus an action which proceeds from irrational fear of the consequences of its omission, has an unhealthy compulsive character. This compulsive-obsessional quality may appear in religious practices, as when there is a ritualistic adherence to the recital of a particular set of prayer formulae, accompanied by an irrational fear of dire consequences if any item of the ritual is omitted.

The misuse of religion to serve neurotic needs was specifically what Freud had in mind in his essays on religion as a neurosis, and what he says is true in certain circumstances. Unfortunately Freud assumed that all religion was to be identified with magical thinking, ritual practices and with the satisfaction of infantile and neurotic needs. There is no doubt that many of the ceremonial and ascetic practices of religion have been and can be used in the service of neurotic needs of individuals or groups. Many people use "religious" behavior as a means to temporal and naturalistic ends, and in extreme cases "religious" activities are manifestations of pathological states. Dependent infantile personalities who have successfully avoided coping with appetites and desires through repression, may also gravitate towards religion. These are

Freud's insights, but partly because of his own personal
history he did not see, or perhaps unconsciously did not
want to see, the fallacy of identifying true religion with
the infantile and neurotic processes.

One area in which a religious exercise can be changed
into an unhealthy process is the area of imagery. Imagery
of a religious kind can be helpful. In persons who are
predisposed to neurotic ways of thinking, however, it
can be an unhealthy alternative to prayer. The image
associated with some doctrines of religion can be emotionally disturbing. Individuals with a volatile emotional
life may feed their emotional life in pathological ways
with imagery, which because it is in the context of religion, seems innocuous. For a disturbed individual imagery
can be too "real." Sometimes the image of the crucifix
in a disturbed mind, dwelt on in a neurotic way, can be
an unhealthy process. The danger here is that the border-
line between love with and love without a sexual component is very tenuous indeed. The person is a psychosomatic unit, so there will be a sensory component in
even the most exalted acts of intellect. The sensory component can, however, get out of hand in the disturbed
personality. An extreme example of this is the case of
the nuns of Loudun in the seventeenth century who suc-
cumbed to an hysterical process. Their very acts of religion were serving a libidinal need. Ritual, symbolism,
incense, music and lights can all be used to foment sensory emotional states. Music, incense and lights are rightly
used as symbolic expressions of the language of worship,
and the fact that a sensory element is involved does not
take from them as worshipful acts. We are after all creatures of sense. Some individuals, however, may become
preoccupied with these aspects of religious ceremonial,
rather than with the reality of religion itself. The ritual-

istic performances of religion and the symbolic expression of worship through sensory means can be a help. The senses need something to occupy them. The other extreme is the elimination of the sensory, as in some religious assemblies where the meeting takes place in a bare room with no symbols. In this situation people may have recourse to "mystical" experiences which may savor of the hysterical. Experiments in sensory deprivation have amply demonstrated that the greater the degree of sensory deprivation the sooner the onset of hallucinatory processes. On the other hand we must guard against the danger of substituting the sensory for intellectual religious content. This is what may happen when what is merely a "sacred concert" is called a "religious ceremony" or a "religious experience." The sensory and the symbolic take over to the exclusion of genuine religious worship.

Some religious practices can present a picture which is closely related to forms of sexual deviation. Ascetic practices (such as the now uncommon use of the discipline or similar penitential practices) can savor of sado-masochism. The danger is that an individual may use an ascetic practice so that it becomes in fact a sexual stimulus. It is a warning-signal if an ascetical practice is accompanied by a fantasy, either a sexual fantasy or even a religious fantasy which may be a distorted sexual fantasy. The flagellantes in the Middle Ages used the practice of the discipline as a neurotic means of achieving a sado-masochistic release. The infliction of pain can be an unhealthy gratificatory process of a sexual kind in some disturbed personalities.

A less serious deviation is the near-obsessional attachment to certain material objects or symbols that may sometimes appear in religious people. Fetishism in the full sense of the term is a disturbance which Freud rightly analyzed as having deep sexual significance. It means the use of objects, not necessarily associated with sexuality, for gratification at deep levels of libido. A mild form of this is the sensory-affective attachment people sometimes manifest, particularly for objects associated with religion. There may be an element of tactile satisfaction in physical contact with the object, although there is no conscious awareness of any kind of sexual gratification. This attachment may be near the threshold of rationality, but it is also related to deep unconscious processes. If objects are regarded merely as religious symbols this is not unhealthy. Symbolism is intrinsic to the human psyche and is therefore characteristic of human religious behavior, because of the psycho-physical nature of the human person. But if a "religious" object becomes a source of sensory gratification, this may be related more to fetishism than to religious symbolism.

It is possible that the use of some symbols well known to psychologists as having an unconscious sexual meaning is sanctioned by the Church by using them in a transmuted way. There is a universal primitive symbolism in water, fire, candles. If the Paschal Candle is divorced from the context of *lumen Christi* it is not far removed from the primitive phallic symbol. Primitive symbols are transmuted by Christianity, but there is a linear continuity from earliest paganism which it is not difficult to recognize. The transmutation elevates the whole process to a higher level but the original symbolism remains. The oral symbolism of communion, the consuming and incorporating of the loved object, can be disturbing, but the agape or love-feast aspect is also there. In many religious activities such as the Eucharist the demands of the psyche are met at several levels: first, the unconscious level of primitive oral needs; secondly, the conscious sensory level which is catered for by the use of the material elements of bread and wine; and finally, the rational level, the level at which the intellectual act of faith is made. The fact that different needs at different levels of the psyche are met in this way, is sometimes used as an argument against religion. On the contrary, however, it would be difficult to accept the truth of any religion which does not take account of the complexities of the human psyche.

Aberrations of religion arise from substituting emotional states for genuine religion, as in the trance-like states of degenerate forms of religious practice. This is nearly always a substitution of organic pleasure for any genuine religious dimension, or alternatively a deliberate fomenting of hysteria. (Cf. Sargant: *Battle for the Mind,* 1957). Ronald Knox in his *Enthusiasm* (1950) also makes the case that most aberrant religious practices come from the substitution of emotional enthusiasm for rational faith. Some so-called "prayer groups" also appear to assume that the psychological functions precipitated by intense emotional states induced in the group activity are "the swift and gracious action of the Spirit." The claim is made by these groups to have received "the Baptism of the Spirit." The only evidence for this is the subjective reports of individuals in states of euphoria, "ecstatic" or "mystical" states, or of the feeling of the "almost intangible presence of the Spirit." Group prayer with an emphasis on emotional aspects appears to be intrinsic to these movements, often accompanied by the imposition of hands and certainly suggesting a close analogue with the so-called snake cults of the southern states of the United States of America. Group prayer *as prayer* can and should be worshipful, but there is an obvious warning-signal in the fact that the experience of the group process seems to have a particular attraction for the emotionally disturbed and the immature.

Puritanism is another faulty religious attitude which is closely related to psychological distortion. Puritanism, Calvinism and Manicheism all regard human nature as something intrinsically evil. As a result all physical and emotional aspects of human functioning, but particularly human sexual love, are regarded as evil and to be repudiated. On the contrary, however, no emotion is wrong or evil in itself. Evil arises only when the emotion is allowed to dominate rationality or when it is given free rein in circumstances where the *right* to experience it is absent.

3. *Religion and Maturity*

It is not the function of religion as such to bring about natural maturation but never the less true religion fully lived should serve as an integrating force in molding the personality and producing complete mental health. True and genuine religion ought to be the voluntary commitment of intellect and will to God, as well as the exercise of rational control in the context of God's commands. A rationally based set of beliefs and practices is intrinsic to maturity. It is not just that in its absence an individual could be equally mature (although maturity is possible without religion). The main problem is not whether it is the function of religion to bring about a higher level of maturity, but why it does not serve this function in certain cases, and why in some cases it seems to be a retarding factor.

It is true that some religions are actually in themselves a retarding influence. They hold people back from the level of maturity they should reach because they are based on the non-rational. Maturity, if it is anything, is the emergence of the rational. If the person is bound to primitive magic, ritual or animistic beliefs, these will necessarily retard the maturation process. There is always a danger that religion may be taught at a non-rational level, for example, in the same sort of context as mythology or fairy-tales, or it may be taught as though its primary function were *edification*. If a set of truths is taught, not because they are true but because they are edifying, the less mature, less intelligent individuals will be kept at a lower level of maturation, while the more intelligent will tend to reject the whole system. The formal function of religion is the worship of God and the sanctification of persons, but it is not the role of religion to produce the mature, well-integrated personality. If immaturity is already a dimension of the individual personality, it is not the function of religion to alter this or to supply for the deficiencies of nature.

On the other hand, religion does not *produce* neurosis or a psychosis. Religion as received by a particular personality may be such that in some of its dimensions it could aggravate an incipient neurosis or psychosis. If an individual is prone to neurotic guilt, his "guilt" may be intensified by certain religious practices. There is often a religious content or background in some forms of mental illness. Inevitably, what is of very great importance in one's normal healthy life will appear in mental illness as the focus of a disturbed thought process. Since religious belief and practice are often the most important elements in normal mental life, it is natural to expect that they will have a corresponding prominence in neurotic and psychotic conditions.

Religion has a social or community aspect. If an individual decides on a private religion with private rituals, this is immediately seen to be in the area of psychopathology. Huxley said that one could be a religious man without any ritual or external manifestation, but this is not possible. One of Freud's insights was his recognition of the ideosyncratic character of a private-ritual type of religion. The practice of religion is a symbolic language expressing, or trying to express more meaningfully than by verbal language, the inner state of the believer. The need for public ritual is intrinsic to man, and because his verbal utterances are an inadequate language. This inadequacy of verbal utterance leads to the notion of the "ineffable," that which cannot be said in words. Instead of words, another dimension of behavior is used: prostrating in worship, symbolic pouring of libation, offering of sacrifice. These are ways of "saying" what vocabulary language is inadequate to say. Apparently, however, verbal utterance is in inverse ratio to religious practices. The more culturally advanced a people is, the more adequate are its utterances and the less organic involvement is necessary. The more primitive the religion, the greater will be the organic involvement.

4. *Scruples and Neuroses*

There are many different conditions, different from each other and different from "scruples" proper, subsumed under the single term "scrupulous." Theologians have long asserted the close connection between the condition called "scruples" and certain forms of mental illness. It would be a mistake to assume that all scruples are forms of mental illness or that all scrupulous people are neurotic. It is worth referring here to the fallacy of *psychomechanistic parallelism*: the fallacy of assuming that where two observable behavior patterns are similar the psychological processes underlying them must be the same.

It is important to recognize in the first instance that scruples in the strict sense are a spiritual trial, a purification, which usually works through a great deal of interior suffering, an agony of doubt and uncertainty about sin or guilt, a meticulous care for and observance of the law. Too often contemporary writers forget that scruples in the strict sense are an "illness of the spirit," which is not the same as a mental illness. In the past probably all similar behavior patterns popularly called "scruples" were thought of as forms of illness of the spirit. But we are in danger of going to the other extreme now and thinking of them all as forms of neurosis or forms of mental illness. Scruples in the strict sense can be thought of as a difficult and painful stage in the process of maturation in the spiritual life. They may serve as a mortification, as a means of deepening one's realization of the spiritual world, and as a means of acquiring docility, humility and self-knowledge. They may also lead to a deepening of faith and trust in God. Unhappily, however, many of the manifestations of scruples are paralleled in the neuroses, so that it is often difficult to decide whether one is dealing with a scrupulous person or with a mentally ill person. What might very well be right and efficacious in the case of "real" scruples might be undesirable indeed in the parallel case of neurotics.

Guilt: To help us to understand the psychology of scruples it is important to make certain distinctions about the notion of guilt. Guilt is the situation whereby the conscious rational adult, judging his own behavior, judges that what he did consciously and deliberately, was a violation of moral law. This is not an emotional reaction but a judgment of the intellect: "I did wrong knowing that it was wrong." This judgment of the intellect on human acts does not occur in a psychological vacuum, but in the context of the *person*, so normally there will occur simultaneously with the judgment an *emotional awareness*, a built-in self-regulating principle which is not itself the judgment of guilt, but an indication that things are out of phase. This is a psychological condition which can be called emotional guilt.

There are really four types of guilt:

(1) First there is *theological guilt*. This is the guilt incurred by an individual who, in addition to the general awareness of wrongdoing, also explicitly or implicitly relates his act to God or to the law of God.

(2) Secondly, there is *natural or rational guilt*. This is the condition of a person who knowingly and willingly violates the natural moral law, even though he does not explicitly advert to the element of transgression of the commandment or the law of God. It is the judgment of the intellect on the human act whereby we decide on the basis of intellectual knowledge that the act was or was not a contravention of law and order.

(3) Thirdly, there is a condition of *normal or healthy emotional guilt*. This is the state of emotions which is experienced when a reasonably balanced person, who is neither hardened to wrong-doing nor pathologically cold, commits a serious sin or transgression of the moral order. For example, it is perfectly healthy and normal for an individual to feel something of this if he commits a violation of the positive law. This is an experience which most people undergo at some time or other. It is not itself "real" guilt, but is a natural concomitant of real guilt, and serves as an

"indicator" that something is wrong in the moral order. It is the normal healthy state of the person in respect of his own acts, an emotional awareness that what he is doing is wrong, even if at times he may not be able to formulate the moral principle involved.

(4) Finally, there is *neurotic guilt*. This is a complex state of the emotions involving dread, anxiety, fear of punishment, desire for punishment, a sense of horror, depression, self-loathing, etc.

(a) It is prolonged through time out of all proportion to its precipitating cause and it can exist without apparent cause.

(b) Usually it is of a degree of intensity which is out of all proportion to its precipitating cause and it can be of such magnitude that it interferes with one's normal adaptation, or produces psychological consequences such as insomnia, loss of weight, morbid suicidal ideas, sweating, anorexia, gastric symptoms.

(c) There is a self-punitive, masochistic component in this state. The individual refuses to accept forgiveness, to be relieved of the guilt. An individual suffering from neurotic guilt will often have incurred real guilt, which he is not prepared to acknowledge, in respect of something else. He uses the emotional guilt then to punish the real guilt.

Among the components of neurotic guilt are fear, dread of nemesis, and also a certain pride, a satisfaction in undergoing this apparent torment. This in turn is accompanied by anxiety, sadness, sorrow and a tinge of despair, some self-directed loathing and perhaps anger.

Emotional guilt, both "normal" and "neurotic," is related to the infantile experience of training, violation of the rules a mother imposes on her child, infantile aggression, destructive impulses, which emerge at a very early age, and many other factors besides. The child, and even more so the infant, can learn to conform to rules, but his behavior is not yet "moral" or "immoral" behavior. Yet it is subject to sanctions. Certain kinds of behavior are acceptable, others are unacceptable. Reward follows on some of them, punishment on others. The child rapidly acquires a set of built-in controls operating at a pre-moral level (i.e. at a level below that of conceptual thinking and judgment), which gives rise to the "feeling" of guilt. In the case of some children these feelings can be very intense and painful. The child's only defence against these painful feelings lies either in rigid conformity so that they will not occur, or in repression so that they may be extruded from consciousness. It is probably here that we find the origin of scruples. For the former process (rigid conformity) is a way of avoiding any experience of guilt-feelings and this may be the source of scruples in the strict sense, while the latter may lead to the neurotic form of scrupulosity: the repressed guilt feelings may remain repressed for a very long time, to emerge again in adolescence or in adulthood, or even in senescence. Thus, probably both real and apparent scruples have their origin in infantile experience. The former mode is describable as genuine scruples, because through the *operation* of this process one may in fact avoid serious wrong doing. But the latter mode (repression giving rise to neurotic processes) is the source of the illnesses so closely resembling scruples.

Compulsive-obsessional neurosis: The illness most closely resembling scruples is compulsive-obsessional neurosis. In this condition the individual suffers from the presence of ideas or images which he cannot root out and which lead to agonies of self-examination, repetitive per-

formance of routine actions, preoccupation with inten-
tion, or with the saying of a particular set of words or
with trivialities which cripple his freedom of action. In
this illness the *form* remains the same for different cases
but the *content* of the obsessional ideas or compulsive
actions is determined by the personal life-history of the
sufferer. Thus the content will be different for a bank
clerk, a professional baseball player, a believing Christian,
a religious. One should look first to the form rather than
to the content. There is no point whatsoever in spending
long hours arguing with such a person about the perform-
ance of duty, the saying of prayers, etc., or in theological
disputes about the mercy and justice of God. If the sufferer were a baseball player there would be no point in arguing interminably with him about the scores of a particular
match, or the reasons why he had missed a particular
catch. The form of behavior is the same, only the content
is different.

Involutional melancholia: Equally impressive is the
condition known as involutional melancholia. This is an
illness specific to the declining years, the late sixties or
early seventies being particularly vulnerable. It is characterized by intense and painful suffering in the mind. In
this senile state immediate memory declines while old
memories are vivid. These old memories may include peccadilloes and sins of youth and generate guilt and fear of
punishment after death. While the sufferer seeks consolation in lengthy discussions with a spiritual director he is
still overwhelmed by feelings of guilt, failure, impending
punishment, etc. He seeks repeated forgiveness and reassurance that he is not going to hell. It can look like a
real theological problem; the sufferer will even hark back
to peccadilloes of infancy or adolescence. But the observer
will notice also marked loss of weight, great melancholy

beyond consolation, insomnia, loss of normal adaptation, etc. This is a curable condition and the sooner a psychiatrist is called the better. (This holds also for the condition of compulsive-obsessional neurosis, though here the amount of help the psychiatrist can give is much less).

Depression and anxiety states: Depression and anxiety states are another set of psychiatric illnesses wherein behavior analogous to scruples may appear. There are two kinds of depression (and we do not here refer to the perfectly normal experience of feeling sad or depressed in an appropriate degree and when the situation provides an adequate cause for the sadness). The first pathological depression is called a reactive depression, for which there is a cause, such as the loss of a parent or loss of one's good name or way of life, but the intensity of the emotion and its duration through time are out of all proportion to the apparent cause. In these cases, also, the criterion must be the degree to which one's normal adaptation is interfered with (for example, a mother who in this situation refuses to care for her children). The other form is endogenous depression. In this condition one feels intolerable sadness, misery, and self-depreciation without any discernible cause in the environment or indeed within oneself. The depression wells up from within. It can be paralyzing and will certainly make it impossible for the sufferer to carry on his normal way of life. It cannot be too strongly stressed that this is a real and definable illness and is amenable to ready treatment. There is no point whatsoever in telling the sufferer to "pull himself together." One might as well tell a sufferer from tuberculosis to heal up his pulmonary lesions. The real danger in this condition is suicide. Suicidal ideas appear only too frequently in this state and it is the opinion of the present writer that most successful suicides are due to endogenous depressions. (Hysterics also attempt suicide but as a symbolic gesture and they rarely go the whole way, or if death does ensue it is because their plan somehow went wrong). Anxiety states characterize the middle years (they are precipitated perhaps by the awareness of declining years, the sense of failure, the unavoidable awareness of impending death). Sufferers from both the depressions and the anxiety states may have recourse to liquor as a way of coping with their condition. The depressed individual gets a temporary relief, the anxiety is temporarily allayed. But there is no cure along these lines and gradually the sheer amount of alcohol must be steadily increased. Both these conditions may precipitate states which closely resemble scruples proper. Thus the depression may be accompanied by a vivid and acute sense of inadequacy. In a religious person, this may appear in the guise of a conversion to spiritual things. But the unhealthy character of the apparent "conversion" will appear in many ways: there will be no real deepening of the spiritual life, no increase of faith or of zeal. Rather the person becomes preoccupied with self, seeking only relief from his condition. The anxieties may be accompanied by a deepening awareness of the last things, but emotional fear with psychological consequences will predominate. It is to be stressed, however, that the consequences for the individual's physical health and the degree to which he cannot sustain his normal adaptation (to job, way of life, obligations, interpersonal relations, etc.) must be the first criterion in deciding whether one is dealing with scruples or with a natural illness.

Hysteria: Some forms of hysteria also resemble scruples. Hysteria is a polymorphous disease. But in general all the many forms in which it appears have one thing in common: a repression of, or fear of, the consciousness of the whole sexual apparatus. The aetiology of hysteria always seems to point to something wrong in the psycho-sexual development of the individual suffering from it. The hysteric may produce wounds resembling stigmata, or see "visions," or appear as a holy person. But equally he or she may become preoccupied with guilt. This will not usually be consciously sexual guilt, because of the repressive mechanism underlying the illness, but may appear in the context of small misdemeanors or things which are not sinful in any way (thus a girl may be full of guilt feelings about her menstrual periods). It is particularly important not to treat such people as scrupulous. They may actually be deriving a vicarious sexual satisfaction from their apparent anxiety and guilt feeling about something harmless or neutral. It is of course even more dangerous to probe for the "real" cause of the guilt feelings, since this will be the same as the root cause of the hysteria itself. The result may only be the release of intense libido which gets rapidly out of control.

"Pseudo"-scruples: There is a common form of near-scruples or pseudo-scruples in adolescence. This is the condition of a youth not otherwise emotionally disturbed who gets very upset about the real state of his conscience. He is clearly earnest but very frightened, worried, anxious, preoccupied with notions of sin, and particularly with the problem of responsibility and consent. This was the condition of Joyce. The youth may try out some rationalizations: "I do not know whether I was awake or not." "I think I did it but. . . ." "I was not sure if it was wrong," etc. Such a boy or girl may be in need of great help. This is not yet scruples and one should be loth indeed ever to allow a young person in the teens to get the idea that he is scrupulous in the strict sense. The case I have just described is the case of someone who perhaps

has been guilty of some form of wrong-doing for some time (very often masturbation) and has succeeded by means of repression in keeping the associated guilt-feelings from consciousness. But as he moves on through the teens the possibility of keeping his real guilt at bay diminishes. This will be particularly true of the more intelligent, the more insightful of this age group. Unconsciously, the adolescent knows that if he once allows the guilt feelings to surface he will have to acknowledge his real guilt, and conversely, if he accepts his real guilt he will have to cope with the most intense guilt feelings. He will therefore try to hold his real guilt at bay, to stave it off. We do not really help such a one by telling him that he is not guilty and is just being scrupulous. He knows very well that he is doing wrong. The approach here, as in so many analogous situations, is to try to help him to accept his real guilt, not to declare him innocent.

All the above conditions have several factors in common and some are also common to "real" scruples. They all seek, not perfection, but self-satisfaction. They all seek, not forgiveness, but a declaration of innocence. They are all states in which the rational conscience is under severe pressure from the pre-rational conscience of the child, operating through *guilt feelings* rather than through *guilt judgment*.

But "real" scruples are not a natural illness. They are a spiritual trial. They may appear in a weak or even childish personality. But the genuinely scrupulous person is really seeking help to advance in the spiritual life. He will retain insight and control simply because the psyche is healthy though perhaps immature, while pseudo-scruples are manifestations of a disturbed psyche. The individual's conscience is under such severe pressure as to be temporarily incapable of decision-making. The scrupulous

person going through the spiritual illness or trial of scruples remains docile, grows rapidly in self-acceptance, is
prepared to suffer (while the analogous natural conditions seek only relief), does not seek self-justification,
and does not manifest morbid somatic symptoms. Pseudo-
scruples have rightly been described as a way of defending
against real guilt, while real scruples are a way of coming
to grips with real guilt, however slight.

CHAPTER III

GRACE, FAITH AND THE HUMAN PERSON

Many of the basic propositions of modern psychology commonly regarded as new were known through the centuries, though in different terminology, to poets, philosophers and ministers of religion. Most psychologists will admit that the degree of comprehension of mind itself, as distinct from a greater insight into various facets of mental life, which modern psychology has achieved is small indeed. Psychology is not a self-contained science and of itself cannot explain the meaning of existence or the purpose of life. Man is not simply a neuromuscular organism, and a purely materialistic psychology is a contradiction in terms. The sciences of the mind demand a synthesis on a higher plane, the plane of religion and philosophy. To omit a consideration of religion in any study of human personality would be to neglect a vast area of human behavior and therefore of human psychology.

The greatest difficulty in all questions related to religion and psychology is to keep clear the distinction between the natural and the supernatural orders of reality.

Two different kinds of problem are involved here:

(1) the empirical observation of natural phenomena associated with religious behavior;

(2) phenomena of the supernatural order which can-

not be explained by natural means, although the assumption is often made that they can be so explained.

1. *The experiential dimension*

Most of the literature in the field of religion and psychology confuses the subjective experiential dimension with the supposedly religious value of this dimension. There is no channel of experience in the religious sphere which is specific to religion. There is no "religious" way of experiencing. There is no "quality" of religious experiences, no definable entity which makes something a religious "thing." It is the "object" of the experience that makes it religious, for example, the fact that prayer is directed to God. The assumption of James (1902), Thouless (1956), Laski (1961), and other authors in this area is that it is the quality of the experience itself that defines it as religious.

The terms *mystical, mysterious, mythical, magical,* etc. are often used interchangeably in a confused way. It must first be pointed out that *mystical* is not the same as *numinous.* The *numinous* refers to the attribution of some non-spatiotemporal property to some spatiotemporal object; so a tree, a statue, a totem pole or any representation of God can be endowed with numinous quality. The term *mystical* is often used wrongly to describe this attribution. Mystical must be used in a very restricted sense. It refers to phenomena which could not be accounted for by anything within the space-time dimension or within human resource.

Marganita Laski (1961) considers under the head of "mystical" the reaction to beauty in art or nature, religious contemplation, experiences of love, and sexual orgasm. She regards all these as forms of "ecstasy" or "mystical experiences." The only problem, she says, is to differentiate the triggering mechanisms, otherwise they are all the same thing. They are all "mystical" in her use of the term because of the quality of the experience. She is here confusing the quality of the experience with the validity of the content. The quality of the experience has in fact nothing to do with its religious value. It is not only *not* a criterion of the religious nature of the experience, but can be misleading, unreliable and totally unrelated to any genuine religious activity. The very phrase "religious experience" is misleading. There is no such thing as a "religious" experience. With regard to religion and psychology, there tend to be two points of view: either that there is a specific kind of experience, called by various names (e.g. Allport's "religious sentiment"), which is the precise object of a special study, or else that there is not, and that therefore religion is a snare and a delusion. It is not a far cry from Freud's *Future of an Illusion* (1928) to Allport's *The Individual and His Religion* (1950).

Rudolf Otto (1923), Friedrich Schleiermacher (apud Johnson, 1959), Allport (1950), James (1902), and others appear to have thought that there is some one or more specifying factors which identify the religious experience: whether it be the sense of oneness, the "holy," the *numinosum*, or any other. James made it possible to speak about a "religious fear," "religious love" and so on as though these more universal emotions could also have a special "religious" flavor. But this would seem to be a mistake. It reduces religion to the irrational or the prerational. It makes it such a subjective phenomenon that it eludes study and makes it possible for a person to reject it totally and become an atheist or an agnostic merely on the ground that these very elusive and deceptive experiences called "religious" have not so far come his way.

Similarly there is a kind of non-cognitive affective experience common to many spheres such as art, beauty, love, etc. Many people think that an experience of this kind is a necessary criterion of religious validity. This idea that one ought to be able to identify the "religious" dimension of an experience is due to a misunderstanding of the nature of grace and the supernatural.

There is no doubt that one finds a common set of factors more or less universally associated with what is called religious experience. Thus we shall expect to find such factors as awe, reverence, love, hope, in all religions. But the reason for this is not so much that they are *intrinsic* to religion but that they are to some extent the consequences of our beliefs, and are often the motivations for religious acts or stimuli for further acts.

Whatever is experienced is a space-time event. The converse of this also holds, *i.e.* nothing that is *not* a space-time event can be experienced. Our channels of experience are limited to the ordinary sensory-perceptual processes. All knowledge comes through these sensory channels. There are no extrasensory channels through which we get special knowledge. Even if there were a sensory channel which was related to extrasensory perception, we would still have to face the implication that this alleged "sixth sense" picking up some unknown radiation emanating from some unknown source would still be operating within the confines of a space-time event. It does not follow that by inventing a concept and calling it a "sixth sense" we are then out of the space-time dimension.

Since the object of our experiencing is always a space-time event, and since only space-time events can be experienced, it follows that if we talk about a "religious experience," meaning an experience of something out-

side space-time, the term is self-contradictory. The tradition of experiential religion is that somehow the events
outside space-time can be brought within space-time and
actually experienced. The sixth sense or "*psi*-phenome-
non" is sometimes alleged to be a carry-over from primitive man who thought he was in direct touch with nature
and the spirit-worlds. From the work of anthropologists
we know that there is a great deal of animism in the
thinking of primitive peoples, but claims to any form
of *psi*-phenomenon or sixth sensory channel have invari-
ably upon investigation proved to be false. As well as the
limitation of the channels of experience there is also a
limitation in the object of our sensory channels. The psychology of sensation, perception, cognition, etc. demon-
strates that stimulus and response are reciprocally related. They are both space-time events related in space-
time.

Introspective reporting is notoriously misleading, so
all claims to have experienced "the divine" or anything
outside space-time must be treated with very great caution. In the absence of convalidating evidence independent of the introspective report, the report has to be relegated to the domain of legitimate doubt, *i.e.* it is not
acceptable evidence for psychology. In Marganita Laski's
argument, since "mystical" experiences occur in sex, contemplation of beauty, etc. then all forms of "ecstasy"
are co-ordinate, *i.e.* of the same order of reality. This
type of thinking either (a) claims that there is no supernatural order, or (b) is unable to distinguish between the
empirical and the supernatural. An example of the latter
confusion is also found in Bertrand Russell. Speaking on
prayer, he once suggested that it should be tested by its
consequences, for example, in an experiment somewhat
as follows: if a hundred children are involved in road

accidents, the efficacy of prayer can be tested by getting the parents of fifty of them to pray and allowing the other fifty to be treated by the best scientific methods. The assumption of Russell (as also of Hume) is that there are only space-time events and they expressly exclude the possibility of extrapolation from within space-time to possibilities outside space-time. There is no point at which it can be said that the only things that exist are space-time events. What can be said is that the only things that can be *experienced* are space-time events. It cannot be said that the only kind of knowledge is sensory knowledge; all that can be said is that sensory channels are the only channels that are related to space-time events.

The contemporary approach to religious matters is very often to assume that what is not "experienced" is not true. This stems from James (1902), who said:

> Religion is the feelings, acts and experience of individual men in their solitude so far as they apprehend themselves to stand in relation to whatever they may consider the divine. (p. 31.)

James' assumption that "religion is the feelings, acts and experience" is the crucial problem here. In saying this James is bringing religion into the domain of the empirical, the observable and the measurable. The feelings, acts and experiences of individuals are not always even evidence of their alleged object. This is clear in the case of pathological states. Indeed, if feelings, acts and experiences subjectively described are the evidence for genuine religion, it will follow that the religious maniac is the most religious of all. This is the consequence pointed out by Erich Fromm (1950) in his account of Jung's psychology of religion. Something more than the "experience" is required. Perhaps the first requirement is evidence of mental health, the level and quality of rationality both of the individual concerned and of the content of the experience. The second requirement will be the spiritual criterion: "By their fruits ye shall know them." If there is evidence of any psychopathology one must withhold any possibility of an explanation in terms of a supernatural phenomenon. (At the same time it must be borne in mind that God can if he wants, use pathological processes). We are, however, only entitled to assent to the possibility of a supernatural source when every other possible explanation is excluded. Suspension of judgment means that while leaving open either possibility we do not give final assent. Rejection is far more often the conclusion in these matters, but suspension of judgment is the more reasonable approach. James' definition includes behavior that could be called "religious" only in one dimension. The person suffering from religious mania may react to things of a religious nature but in no sense could his behavior be called "religious" behavior.

The psychology of "mystical" experience when considering the felt dimension, will necessarily regard it in terms of the only known channels of experience. When people try to describe the nature of religious experience with words like "unity," "timelessness," "ineffability," etc. this seems merely to emphasize the point that we have only the normal channels of experience and therefore cannot apprehend anything *outside the space-time continuum*. Psychology as such cannot solve the problem of the authenticity or otherwise of a religious experience.

(1) Psychology can only talk about the experience itself and gives no criteria for evaluating the *content* of the experience.

(2) The most important supernatural realities, God, faith, grace, sin, cannot be experienced at all.

This gives rise to the question of whether or not there can be a psychology of religion. In most works the "religious" dimension of an experience is assumed to be the subject-matter of a psychology of religion. But the content and quality of an experience is not the evidence of its religious character or validity. In the cases of Joan of Arc and Teresa Neumann we have the phenomenon of hearing "voices." In both cases the experience is describable as a purely psychological phenomenon. The problem is how to distinguish whether or not a phenomenon of this kind is a genuinely religious occurrence or a pathological manifestation. This cannot be done by any psychological means.

The difficulty here can be put in another way. Since our channels of experience are limited and since introspective reporting is notoriously difficult, it will not be surprising to find many forms of experience, such as poetry, beauty generally, human love, nature, described in much the same terms by different people. Who will arbitrate, and on what grounds? No independent observer can have access to the privileged domain of private awareness of the person who claims and describes any particular experience. And yet we do apply some criteria to decide between the "experiences" of the psychotic or neurotic on the one hand and the healthy personality on the other. Thus we distinguish fairly easily between the hallucinatory voices of the schizophrenic and the ordinary experience of hearing another human voice, but the distinction does not lie within the experience. When it comes to the psychology of religion, however, even the best psychologists are inclined to ignore this fundamental issue. Freud is usually thought of as the arch-priest of the theory that the reality of religion had been exploded once and for all by showing that it was a form of neurosis (fallacy of psychomechanistic parallelism). But Freud's efforts to eliminate religion by identifying it with neurotic processes was in no sense related to the truth or otherwise of religious beliefs. Their content was not accounted for by the history of how we might have come to think of them.

It is important to note that one cannot study the psychology of religion while adopting a totally detached or agnostic view about the content of religious beliefs. This point of view remains wholly within the domain of this world and might indeed legitimately be called a psychology of religious behavior but not of religion. If one adopts this point of view, then Freud's explanation is the only valid approach: such behavior is the behavior of the psychotic, the neurotic or the child.

2. *Frames of Reference*

There are two contrasting views of man and his world, two frames of reference, the "naturalistic" and the "theological." To many people these two ways of viewing the world seem to be contradictory or mutually exclusive.

The naturalistic frame of reference sees man as belonging wholly to the space-time continuum, to be studied exclusively by the methods with which we study the rest of the material world. According to this way of thinking, only such propositions as are admissible about the material world are admissible about man. And all such propositions are subject to the same methods of observation and verification as apply to the material world. The naturalistic viewpoint sees no place for grace, faith or eternal values in the scheme of things. Man is at the center of his world and his human perfecting becomes the supreme goal. This point of view becomes intelligible when one remembers that questions about man, society,

grace, faith and eternal values are among the most difficult the human mind can ask. Confronted with problems
of such magnitude, the temptation is to over-simplify,
perhaps to "reduce" one element to another as one tries
to do in the physical sciences: to "reduce" intellect to
"sense," will to emotion, religion to neurosis, grace to nature. While the "naturalistic" viewpoint cannot see the
place of faith, grace or values, at the same time these
words are regarded as too valuable to lose. They are retained therefore, but their meaning is translated into
something comparable to the logic of empiricism. Thus
faith becomes perhaps the relatively simple confidence in
man's ability to solve his own problems, or to improve
himself or his society, or the more subjective concept of
a pseudo-mystical inarticulate felt state of conviction.
The repeated attempts to translate the concept of the
morally good into experienced states of pleasure, happiness, usefulness, or attitudes of approval or disapproval,
illustrate the point from another angle. Moore's point
(1903) that the morally good simply disappears in any
such attempt to translate it into natural terms has still
to be learned by theologians who study society and by
social scientists and psychologists who study religion.

Side by side with the "naturalistic" point of view the
most important realities, God, spirit, grace, faith, sin,
guilt, are totally outside the range of human experience
and perception through the ordinary sensory channels.
Man also differs essentially from the rest of the organic
world in as much as a vital part of him can escape the
limitations of the space-time continuum. The theological
world view which accepts the reality of grace and the
supernatural will not lead to any new observations of
phenomena not made by the naturalistic view, nor will
grace of itself cure our temporal ills: poverty, famine,

war, ignorance, illness. This is the task and privilege of human persons using ordinary human techniques. It is not grace as a force in the world (which it is not) which relieves famine and brings about economic well-being. It is human persons acting under the influence of grace. The theological view sometimes feels threatened by the naturalistic or humanist viewpoint. The very notion of "humanism" has become a danger-signal to some, instead of being at the very heart of religion because of the Incarnation. The theological world-view appears at times to seek refuge in the supernatural, attributing to grace, for example, a causality which it does not possess to solve problems on the natural plane. The theological viewpoint has also tried at times to over-simplify the relationship of nature to the supernatural order of reality. It has done this in two ways: on the one hand it has seemed to bring grace, faith, even God, within the domain of the empirical, *i.e.* these realities are described as capable of being experienced by us in some fashion in our present mode of existence. It can be called the attempt to "reduce" grace to nature. The other device the theological viewpoint sometimes adopts is the topological opposite of this: it is an attempt to "elevate" nature to grace. Although topologically opposed, these two theological viewpoints are identical in essence: according to both, grace and nature belong somehow to the experienceable domain and are one in the long run. Fitting grace into the temporal order as though it were a phenomenon in some way co-ordinate with other temporal phenomena leads inevitably to the acceptance of the "naturalistic" viewpoint. This is the position of those theologians who seek to base their faith either on some form of religious experience or intellectual insight, or more usually perhaps on some form of experience from within the human psyche or of human goodness. This last is the empirical criterion most often applied by young onlookers at the world scene: if they cannot see enough human goodness to satisfy their felt needs they are tempted to withhold their assent of faith.

We are not constrained to accept the "naturalistic" world view, which in fact is not a conclusion from science but an assumption implied by the acceptance of the very methodology which it is claimed establishes it. Nobody has the right to tell a man that his mind must stop short at phenomenological description, however accurate and important. Description is never explanation except on one hypothesis, *viz.* that there is no explanation, no way of understanding, and that the description is its own explanation. The first world view, the "naturalistic" view, does not eliminate the second, the "theological" view, but requires it. If we eliminate the theological view it means doing violence to the clearest and most important facts we know about ourselves: that we are persons, that we make choices, that we are responsible people. It is not a question of choosing exclusively the one view or the other, since each has need of the other. It is a question of "both - and," not of "either - or." The two frames of reference must be combined so that we can state that everything that can be seen, everything capable of being experienced will be describable without remainder in the temporal frame. But the other frame is also indispensable, for the very simple reason that what we see in the temporal frame remains unintelligible without the theological frame. Choosing to see reality through the theological frame of reference is one way of establishing the intelligibility of the whole.

The two world views, the naturalistic and the theological, are seen by some to be unrelated and any discussion of them to be unimportant. The naturalistic view is assumed to be correct and the other is dismissed *a priori* as fanciful or illusory. But it is possible that nobody holds consistently or exclusively to the naturalistic viewpoint. Russell is a case in point: he attempts to uphold values which are negated by his own philosophy; to reject the materialism which is inherent in his own very words. The reason why it is so impossible to hold consistently and exclusively to the naturalistic viewpoint is fairly simple. If it could be established and consistently held, it would have the gravest effects on our world. Perhaps a relatively recent occasion on which the naturalistic viewpoint was logically and inexorably carried through to its conclusions was at Dachau and Belsen. Its effects are also discernible in some contemporary cultures in legalized abortion and demands for legislation of euthanasia.

3. Faith

Faith does not lie in the acquisition by the intellect of the knowledge of the content of religion; any individual can become an expert in Zen Buddhism, Hinduism, Catholic Theology, or any body of doctrine, without necessarily subscribing to the beliefs of that religious system. The intellectual aspect of religious faith is secondary, because it is only a question of acquisition of matter. Faith itself is the *choosing of a frame of reference*. It is the formal factor that infuses, colors or animates the whole, and there is no criterion outside itself whereby one can establish it or lead an unbeliever to accept it. Faith is a condition antecedent to, not a consequence of, the meaning of events in the space-time continuum. Faith is not the end result, so to speak, of an honest inquiry into the authenticity of scriptures, etc. Such an inquiry may indeed be important but it does not automatically attain or guarantee faith. To put this in its most extreme form: one does not find faith as a result of accepting scripture as authentic revelation, simply because in order to accept that it is a revelation one must already have faith. In the same way, reading scripture as the history of salvation is not the way to faith, since one must have chosen faith as the frame through which to see scripture as the history of salvation. The frame of reference is the initial consent of the person to the reality of things unseen. It is not a simple assent of the intellect, because the intellect is constrained by evidence to give its assent. The intellect cannot withhold its assent in the face of evidence.

If faith were simply a matter of a simple assent on evidence to the truth of some proposition, the doctrines of faith would become scientifically verifiable, and thus there would be no room for faith. Neither is it just a consent of the will, although it is a choosing. We lack a third word but it can be put as follows: it is the consent of the *person*, who brings about, as it were, the consent of his intellect to the reality of things unseen. This is the frame of reference. This is possible only through the operation of grace. "Flesh and blood have not revealed this to you, but my Father who is in heaven" (Mt 16:17).

One confusion prevalent in this area is the idea that faith is somehow an experienced state of certitude or conviction. There is a confusion between the certainty of the truth in itself and the subjective state of certitude whereby an individual holds a truth. Faith is neither subjective conviction nor experienced certitude but may indeed be at its best where doubt exists. In former ages when all events were seen "in the light of faith" (in the "age of faith" as the mediaeval centuries have been called), it was easy to see how faith could be thought of as underpinned, even sustained by appeals to empirical phenomena. In our milieu, however, as more and more phenomena are brought under the analysis of the rationalist and scientist, we are coming closer to the opportunity for the pure act of choice. This means that we must take courage to do two things: first, to concede the temporal, the operation of secondary causes, wherever this is possible; to eliminate magic, primitive thinking, mythology, and fear at all levels; to eliminate the "preternatural"; and secondly, in teaching religion to young people to elicit instead the formal act of faith. It is difficult for a generation which thought that it grounded its own faith on fixed sure certainties to recognize that it is the very absence of such certitude which makes the faith of the contemporary believer so much more valuable. The free choice of faith without subjective certainty or felt state of conviction, is in itself a more mature and more valuable thing than a faith based on any kind of presumed evidence.

Contemporary philosophy of education insists at all levels on giving assent based on evidence only. The child is taught to take nothing on trust or on authority in the sciences and in the historical disciplines. In subjects where evidence of this order is not available, for example in literature or contemporary affairs, the pupil is taught to "express his own opinion and give reasons for it." This is intrinsically good but in the question of religious doctrine a distinction must be made between knowledge grounded in evidence, opinion based on probabilities, and belief in non-verifiable truths. It is misleading to imply or to assert that there is a possibility of evidence, empirically verifiable, similar to the kind of evidence used in the sciences, upon which belief may be grounded; that somebody, somewhere, has another dimension, another

facet of experience which guarantees that there is a supernatural order of reality. There is nothing in the spiritual
sphere experienceable or discernible which is not a dimension of an event in the space-time order; a state of
feeling, an act of the will, an act of knowing, desiring,
etc. If the phrase "things unseen" is really understood
we shall realize that there cannot be evidence. There is
no test which can be applied which will provide sensory
evidence in the temporal order upon which belief in the
supernatural order could then be predicated: if there
were this kind of evidence there would be no room for
faith. Faith is an act of free choice of the reality of
"things unseen." It is still a choosing on the ground of
the possibility of the non-experienceable. When the choice
is made this becomes for the believer the frame of reference, the perspective through which everything is subsequently viewed.

Under pressure from phenomenology and existentialist
thinking, theologians in recent years would seem to have
yielded to the temptation to bring faith, grace, sin and
even God himself within the domain of what can be
experienced. If we think of grace and sin as ontological
states of the person rather than empirical phenomena,
many problems can be solved.

4. Grace

According to Catholic doctrine, grace is an analogical
but real participation in the divine existence. It is not
enough for man to live a natural being or by a natural
existence; he has to live in addition at a supernatural level
by participation in the divine life, and this is the com-
pleteness of his existence. When the human organism
begins to be, *i.e.* at the moment of the fertilization of the

ovum, it has a natural existence. In the same moment, *i.e.* without any time interval, its natural existence is replaced by a spiritual existence. At baptism the spiritual existence is replaced by a supernatural existence. This supernatural existence is the life of grace, the analogous participation in the divine existence. By grace the inner mode of the person's existence is changed, though all observable dimensions remain as before. The whole reality of the person's existence is now on a different plane. Because of the reciprocal relationship between person and act (the person performs the act but the act affects the person), grace transforms the acts of man by transforming their source. But there are no discernible effects or consequences of grace in the spatio-temporal order. Grace has no efficacy as an efficient cause in the natural order.

Sin, like grace, is not a phenomenon which can be experienced. It is an ontological condition of responsible creatures. Sin is not the act done as a physical event in space-time but it is the state or condition of a person acting formally as a person in his causal relation to a particular kind of act. The act can be intrinsically evil, but sin lies only in the person's producing such an act when he acts in his formal status as a person.

The psychologist and sociologist, while studying the phenomena of their respective sciences, will not observe the supernatural. What they study will be the same from the observer's point of view whether or not they accept a supernatural order of reality. An individual in the state of grace will not have a higher IQ than one who is not in grace. The relation between grace and the emotions is not such as automatically to weaken their intensity or eliminate their effects on judgment or behavior. Reaction times are not lessened nor learning rates quickened by grace in the soul. Where then will the difference lie? It lies in the whole transformed reality, but not in any observable dimension of it.

The theological world view which accepts the reality of grace will not lead to observations within the world which the natural scientist will not be able to perceive. We are limited in the nature and range of our senses. Our channels of experience are few. What difference does the supernatural order make to the observable? Grace and the supernatural leave everything observable as it was, though they open up whole new worlds of inferential knowledge. Peter Fransen puts it clearly:

> The sciences remain undisturbed by the theology of grace as long as they keep to the investigation and ascertaining of fixed laws and relations among the same specific phenomena. . . . (Fransen, 1968, p. 238.)

The believing physicist will not perceive anything within his science which the unbeliever will not see. He will not have a private revelation to help him understand the observed. The psychologist and the sociologist will not observe grace in the world. It will not be a datum for their sciences. The behavior of a man talking with the tongues of angels and having charity will not have an observable dimension different from similar behavior on the part of one who has not charity. And yet the whole reality will be different. Grace leaves everything exactly as it was and at the same time changes everything utterly. But the change is in the innermost nature, the very beings of things, not in their observable measurable components. It has to be inferred, deduced, assented to.

In our customary appeal to experience we are tempted to place grace, and even God himself, in the context of human affairs, as though grace were simply another phenomenon coordinate with the rest. If this were so it would be susceptible to the same methods of study as the rest, but then grace would not be grace any more. Yet this in a manner of speaking is what the psychologist and sociologist are tempted to do. This is what differentiates a genuine psychology of religion from religious psychology, sociology of religion from *sociologie religieuse*. We are always in danger of limiting the real to the perceptible. But the most important realities of all are precisely those that are not perceptible or even imaginable. They are conceivable. We see only in a clouded mirror. Thus faith, grace, sin and guilt are not experienced dimensions of the human psyche—they are conditions of soul and must be inferred. Only that which is in the natural order can be experienced.

Human behavior is in principle describable within the canons of empirical investigation in purely physical terms. But this is to miss its essential nature as human behavior. It is as though a man lifting a weight and a crane lifting the same weight through the same distance and using the same energy were doing the same thing. The elements of purpose, choice, consciousness, the living reality, are all lost. The same thing can be seen even more clearly if we think about a computer. The computer and man may carry out a task which seems to be the same task in many respects. But when the computer carries out the task, the innermost nature of the human act of thought is lost, that is, its immanent conscious character. The point to note then is that although in perceptible terms the two phenomena may be describable in the same terms, they are never the less essentially distinct, though they may not be distinct in any observable or measurable respect as far as the onlooker is concerned.

Grace inheres in the very being of the soul. It transforms the acts of man by transforming their source, not by adding some further dimension to them. But we have become accustomed to thinking of grace as a felt experience, forgetting that its reality lies too deep for conscious observation. The addition of the dimension of grace no more adds to the list of the perceptible elements of a phenomenon than does its human conscious purposive character. The addition of grace transforms utterly the reality, yet not in any sensory way that the onlooker can observe. Just as human consciousness in another must be inferred not observed, and will not be inferred if it is antecedently eliminated by the rules of the game, (as for example, in behavioristic psychology), in the same way the reality of grace must be inferred, assented to, on grounds other than observation, and moreover on grounds other than those that would suffice for the inferring of consciousness. If grace were implied by the evidence, it would itself belong in the world of sense. We have not here even the dimension of subjective experience of our own, which we have in the case of consciousness.

5. *Social Aspects of Religious Behavior*

One must ask how could these things be studied as a psychology of religion by one who prescinds altogther from the validity of theological formulations? If one consistently prescinds from the validity of such formulations, it seems that one is confronted with an insuperable difficulty. For now the act of belief will be irrelevant or illusory. Motivations, the highest perhaps of which we are capable, will be irrelevant or deceiving.

An essential form of human motivation which is both an ultimate principle in personality integration and an important factor of social organization, as Salman (1965) puts it, will be either irrational or meaningless. If one can legitimately prescind from the content of religious belief it would appear that inevitably one must treat of religious behavior minus its most important component: not the "belief" that it is true but the "fact" that it is true. For Jung all religious propositions have psychological truth, the truth that somebody believes them. But the essential point here is something very different: it is because man *knows* something, and not because he *feels* something, that religion is important psychologically. This is not just the sociologists' dictum that "if men define situations as real, they are real in their consequences" (Thomas, 1951) for if it were only that, it would be our duty to warn people about the delusions involved. A valid psychology of religion will study not just the emotional and other felt states associated with religious experience, but will try also to study the motivations which lead on to and those which seem to block the assent of faith. But if one prescinds from the objectivity or possible truth of faith, all such assents will seem irrational. Similarly a valid research in the field of religion will not limit itself to working out the percentages at different age levels who still go to Church, and differentiating between Roman Catholic and others in this regard. This is not psychology of religion any more than similar figures for attendance at football matches or the theatre would be psychology of football or drama. But it would be important to try to know if the behavior patterns of Catholics differ consistently from those of other religions and if so why; why the small sects in the Deep South of U.S.A, seem to be so emotional, why personality changes can take place with such rapidity in the sphere of religion, with a rapidity not seen elsewhere.

In the sociology of religion the same or similar considerations hold. The mere study of religious behavior (defined perhaps as behavior of a society or its members in terms of religious affiliation) will not present any dimensions different from the behavior of any other social group. The difference will be in the inner reality, the motivations, the effects of belief on the social scene. In the context of individual religious behavior, the real problems arise in the attempt to study the effects, if any, that a man's beliefs have on his behavior, not the study of the behavior as such. The study of the behavior as such is no more religious psychology than the study of any other dimension of behavior. In a similar way the study of the behavior of the social group will not be religious sociology. But there is a vast and exciting area of real religious sociology to be studied; for example, a comparative study of two societies, matched for the usual variables but differing in some definable respect. Take, for example, two comparable social groups, one of which believes in the sacredness of the person, and the other in the expendability of the person in terms of some short term gain. It would be of the utmost importance to study the effects of this difference in real values on other important aspects of such a society. In the same way research into the behavior of Catholics in church attendance is not nearly as important as would be the investigation of the relations between such behavior and on the one hand the observance of the law, and on the other the relation between it and the convictions of the practitioner.

It is often thought that the psychologist's analysis of human behavior has relieved man of responsibility for his behavior. He is either the plaything of unconscious forces or perhaps a set of reflex arcs. It is also widely believed that an understanding of social phenomena leads to the same conclusion. The argument from psychology is based either on the study of unconscious motivation (the analytic schools) or on the study of behavior (the behaviorism of Watson, Tolman, Eysenck). Eysenck reduces man to a collection of behavior patterns, genetic and acquired. There can be no room in this scheme of things for the concepts of responsibility, right and wrong, grace or sin. Others seem to see no essential difference between the behavior of man and that of the white rat. Differences of degree are conceded but no difference in kind, in the quality of the whole, no difference between the nonresponsible act of the animal and the responsible act of the human being. This manner of thinking appears in sociology. Lady Wootton (1959) expressed it in her own way in her suggestion that it is time we got rid altogether of the notion of responsibility. The argument here usually takes some such form as the following: Since we know the conditions in which delinquency occurs (*e.g.* broken homes, poverty, ignorance), and since we know that altering these conditions for the better reduces or eliminates such delinquency, it follows that the individuals who carry out delinquent acts are not responsible for their behavior. This sort of thinking is then applied widely, perhaps to such problems as suicide, unmarried mothers, vandalism, criminal acts, and ultimately the whole range of human behavior.

The theological worldview will not be able to find a new set of events to observe, which eludes the naturalistic view. It will not discover any necessary relation between the criminal act and its consequences. Crime sometimes pays. Syphilis does not always follow sexual indulgence. Insanity does not follow masturbation. And prosperity is not the reward of faith, virtue and religious observance, if one compares the believing nations with the unbelieving. But the theological worldview will wonder at the adequacy of an interpretation of existence which seems to exclude one's own experience of human things from the world and which seems to give no adequate account of some important aspects of human life. It becomes important therefore to ask: what does the naturalistic worldview add up to, and how far is one constrained to accept it? Is it established? Does it give an account of human behavior?

The natural sciences are by their very definition limited to the naturalistic viewpoint. It is vital to their progress to hold to the principle that only the observable is datum for them, and the only explanation of the observable acceptable to them must itself be at least in principle observable. The very history of the natural sciences can be summed up as the consistent and on the whole successful attempt to eliminate the unobservable in their search for explanation. "Observable" in this context means of course "observable at least in principle by an independent observer" other than the person claiming to have made the observation. It is still logically possible that there might be other true propositions not entailed or implied by the propositions of the natural sciences or guaranteed by the canons of natural scientific experiment. If there are such propositions their verification will not lie within the methodology of natural science. Such propositions, if indeed there are such, will be propositions of philosophy and theology.

There are still survivals of Hobbes and Rousseau in our world. The Hobbes point of view is represented by such ideas as that our socialization and humanization are at best only a refuge from a worse misery, processes of a purely instrumental value. Rousseau survives among those who think that socialization in the sense that we are using the term is a dehumanizing process rather than a humanizing one. The concept of *anomie* aptly sums up both points of view in practice. But most people would agree that society, civilization, is a good, a value, intrinsic and objective, though an intermediate one, and that it is a condition of our growth. It is necessary not for short-term satisfactions but for long range realization of potentialities, and thus is as necessary for becoming human beings as oxygen and protein. But where does grace come in?

The apparent paradox of growth in personal stature and responsibility through the limitation of freedom in society has been a fruitful source of speculation among philosophers down the ages. It is also one of the great theological watersheds between Roman and other Christian Churches. It is often forgotten that a Church is a society (it is of course much more than this, but it is at least this), and it will therefore exibit in its life all that one finds to be true of any society as such. One might indeed apply some of the insights of social psychology and group dynamics to the concept of the Church and state some interesting principles. Thus, the more a Church is a society the more will the principle of cohesiveness apply (the principle which states that the more difficult it is to become a member of a given society, the more one feels identified with the society), and the greater the limitation on the freedom of the members. In fact the relationship between growth in personal stature on the one hand and the limitation of freedom of the individual on the other is the crucial problem for educators, political scientists, sociologists, economists at all times.

The concept of "forcing a man to be free" is not as absurd as it seems at first sight. Perhaps the paradox can be resolved very simply. The realization of one's full potentialities as a human being involves the release of rational functioning from the dominance of non-rational or sub-rational factors. The curbing by society is thus seen to be the curbing of one sector of human behavior, the non-rational. Socialization and humanization are seen as liberations and as sources of enhanced responsibility. Do we not hold a man to be more responsible because of the better education he has had? And do we not excuse sometimes on the ground that "he never had a chance because of his background and lack of education"? But the very distinction of rational and non-rational is out of fashion. Some such distinction is, however, necessary whether it be in terms of releasing the "ego" and generating the superego, to handle the problems of the "id," or in terms of "conditioning" the genetically determined behavior patterns so that they become socially acceptable. What does the ego do if it does not think and evaluate? And who or what determines what behavior patterns are going to be determined in what direction and how? The important point is simply this: that there can be neither problem nor answer about human conduct unless some distinction along these lines is maintained. For "behavior" as such is as neutral as any other event in the space-time continuum. But whatever it is that enables us to speculate about these things is what we mean by the rational. Ayer (1963) has contended that "the word 'rational' can be used and is indeed most commonly used, as a term of value" (p. 485). This is not only true but inescapable and is implicit in education, legislation and psychiatry in all their forms. The questions the undergraduate asks in every age: "But why should I be rational?" "Why should I think rationally?" must be answered but not in instrumental or utilitarian terms. The answer is that while one can do otherwise and remain a living organism, one cannot do otherwise and remain human. But why should one remain human? One cannot establish on humanist grounds alone the value of being human. Humanism assumes that being human is itself a value. It follows that there are values necessarily involved in human society, since society is a necessary means for our humanization.

A theological worldview clearly involves the categories of good and evil, right and wrong. But it has seemed to some that the psychological and sociological study of man have no room for such categories. The naturalistic worldview eschews any importation of values into science. Yet it is difficult to believe that those who hold the naturalistic view are really as opposed to these ideas as they appear verbally to be. With Hume and Ayer, they have confused a methodology of investigation with the result of philosophical analysis. It could be argued that all Hume's conclusions are already implicit in his method of testing the validity of ideas against their sensory "impressions" (1817), and all Ayer's conclusions are implicit in the "principle of verification," however formulated (Ayer, 1946). Something similar has happened in other sectors of the intellectual life. If one sets up a particular method of investigation as the only legitimate one (*e.g.* quantification of phenomena and observation under controlled conditions) one is not entitled as a result of the consistent observation of this canon to conclude that there is nothing else to observe. For this does not follow from the findings but is assumed by the principle of method. In much the same way one can say that the principle of sensory empiricism (summarized perhaps in the words: *there are only sensory objects and there is only sensory knowledge*) is not a conclusion, since neither of these propositions could ever be proved, but is a principle of method within one area of speculation. This can be said without prejudice to the truth or falsity of such propositions. The only point at issue at the moment is the logical difference between propositions which are the methodological assumptions of science and those that constitute the findings of science. One of the clearest examples perhaps is the assumption of a thorough-going mechanistic hypothesis by the biologist as a methodological principle of investigation. But many think it is a scientific conclusion. In the human and social sciences, value-free propositions are a methodological assumption, not a scientific finding. One reason for the difficulties of these sciences is that by their assumption of this principle they have turned themselves into descriptive rather than explanatory sciences, more akin to "natural history" or "contemporary history" than to science proper.

In the sciences of man it seems clear that the release of the rational functions, however defined, from the pressures of non-rational forces is only a beginning. There still remains the task of building a mature person, man as he ought to be, and the perfecting of this through grace. And already in the use of the word "ought" we have left the domain of the natural sciences. There is indeed a current methodology which would forbid us to talk about "ought" or to ask about "a man as he ought to be." Once again this methodology is presented as though it were a conclusion, whereas it is an assumption. This is the point of view which would say that "telling men that they ought to live in accordance with their real nature" is really only telling them to do what they do. The words are Ayer's (1963). It is a mistake, he thinks, to "claim that men ought to live in such and such a way because such and such is their real nature." How men actually behave shows their real nature, and if they behaved differently "they would thereby show that they had a different nature." (pp. 479, 480) But this is a confusion of language, an elementary fallacy. Realizing a potentiality is not changing a nature but achieving it. The principle assumed here by Ayer is that of the naturalistic worldview: everything about man must be stated and explained in terms of the same methodological principles which apply to the rest of the observable world. A modified version of this principle is indeed true, *viz.*, the same methodological principles which apply to the rest of the observable world should be applied where possible to find out the facts about man and to explain them, in so far as these principles can do so. But this is a very different principle. And to say that they have not explained everything as yet but will do so in the future is to base a whole philosophy of man on what has been called "the phenomena revealed by hope." It is not surprising that a philosopher or scientist who accepts the first version of the principle ends up with a science about man which contains only positivistic empiricist propositions. Manifestly this is not so because only such propositions are true, or could be established, but simply because only such propositions can be dredged up in the mesh of the net he has chosen to cast. It is sophistical to present them as though they were the only logically possible conclusions. They are the only possible conclusions within a self-imposed logic and that is all. If they are not found to be wholly satisfactory, and if no more satisfactory conclusions can be arrived at within that logic, scientific integrity requires the conclusions that we need a different logic, a wider methodology. Merleau-Ponty saw this clearly. The contemporary sociologist lives in "the blinders of Baconian or Millian induction"; according to Merleau-Ponty, he imposes these "blinders" on himself "even if his own investigations bypass, as it would appear, these

canonic recipes." In other words, he requires of himself
that he stay within his adopted methodology even if the
facts themselves transcend it. "He will pretend to face the
social world as if it were alien to him, as if his study were
not indebted to the experience he has, as a social subject,
of intersubjectivity." (1963, p. 489). The social sciences
and philosophy still doggedly wear the "blinders" of
Bacon and Mill.

CHAPTER IV

PSYCHOPATHOLOGY AND MYSTICAL PHENOMENA

1. *Semantic Difficulties*: *"Mystical"* and *"Mysticism"*

The greatest difficulty in practice in considering psychical, psychological and mystical phenomena is not, as one might suppose the inherent difficulty of the subject-matter but rather the purely semantic one of knowing what one is talking about. Words are used in psychological and mystical literature which seem to be the same as those of ordinary intelligent speech, but on examination it emerges that the objects they denote are very different. The word *mystical* illustrates the point fairly well. (cf. chapter III, p. 58 ff.) Too often it is used as the logical contrary of real, or clear, or literal, or a combination of these, while a mystic is confused with a visionary, and a visionary in turn is taken to be one who is too ethereal to be occupied with mundane affairs or too idealistic to seek for an attainable ideal. Most people, it would seem, confuse mystical with mythical or mysterious, while many seem to think that it has something to do with "misty," as in the phrase "a misty day" when visibility is low and the outlook obscure. The whole problem is still further obscured by the use of "mystical" to describe certain poets or certain kinds of poetry. A poet is not a mystic because his poetry is about abstract or theological con-

cepts, nor even because it seems to derive from a supernatural interpretation of sensory experience, as in Joseph
Mary Plunkett's "I see His blood upon the rose," but
only if the content of the poems he writes is the result of
an inspired experience wrought by the Holy Ghost in his
intellect and will, as in St. John of the Cross. It is scarcely
necessary to add that being a visionary has nothing whatever to do with abstract painting, or El Greco landscapes,
or fortune-telling, or adolescent dreams of youths with
arms outstretched silhouetted against the rising sun. Being a visionary means seeing visions and seeing visions has
a lot in common with the phenomena of illusion, hallucination and imagery. Being a mystic, on the other hand,
need not include seeing visions or being suspended in
mid-air in ecstasy. Being a mystic means being a soul so
purified that intellect and will are subjected to the power
of the Holy Spirit, who infuses a mode of prayer and
sometimes a degree of knowledge which the unaided human being does not achieve. This can and does take place
without the extraneous and unnecessary aid of visions and
"interior voices." The *mystical* means the operation of
the Holy Spirit in the soul. The Holy Spirit is always
operating when we pray, so the mystical is normal in the
Christian life, but so-called "mystical" experience is not.

The only valid definition of the *mystical,* if there is
a reality other than this world, is that it is the operation
of the Holy Spirit in our souls. Otherwise it would seem
that it must refer either to the emotional overtones or
to the content of the experience. For a person who does
not believe in a supernatural order there can be no mysticism, or else the mystical comes within the canons gov-
erning the domain of the sensory. This is perhaps the
reason why so much that is called the psychology of religion is misleading, and why so many who treat the mysti-

cal as though it could be investigated by empirical means
fall back on some doctrine of extrasensory perception.
The mystical, if it occurs, will occur through ordinary
channels of experience. The manifestation of the mystical
in visions, voices and so on, will occur in the spatio-
temporal order. The result is that the account given of
such phenomena from the inside by the experiencer is
not evidence as such of their source. Psychapathology
and mysticism are very close in their manifestations. In
the case of genuine mystical experience all the deficiencies
a person may have in his personality or psyche will remain with him. The inadequacies and idiosyncrasies of
the individual will still be apparent. The content of the
"experienced" will be colored by the natural personality
characteristics and cultural formation of the person
claiming such an experience. In the same way, but conversely, a disturbed personality may cloak the manifestation of his morbid condition in a religious dress. The mentally ill person may manifest behavior which in the terminology of the psychologists who write about these things
will be called "religious," at least it may appear to conform to all the criteria they demand: depersonalization,
unity of consciousness, timelessness, spacelessness, dereali-
zation, sense of peace, ineffability, and so on. On the other
hand, the behavior of the genuinely religious person may
show all the signs of the pathological. St. Joan of Arc
may be represented as an hallucinated young girl who was
also a transvestite. The point to be stressed is that the behavioral dimension may be described without remainder
and yet without any implication of, or reference to, the
religious in any sense in which this term can be meaningfully used. In other words, the behavioral dimension is
not the full story nor is the supposedly religious content
of a "mystical" experience any guarantee of its genuine-

ness, nor is the "goodwill" of the person concerned to be
accepted without question as evidence.

With regard to the phenomena of mysticism in its
proper sense (inspired contemplation), psychology and
psychopathology have nothing positive to contribute, and
for the very good reason that infused contemplation is
brought about by grace, which does not destroy but
perfects and elevates the natural capacities. But in the
other field, that of visions and revelations, they have an
important role to play, and many of the so-called mystical phenomena closely resemble certain phenomena in
the psychopathological dimension. Gabriel (1950) recog-
nizes this. His purpose is to delineate the function of
visions and revelations in the spiritual life rather than
to expound their nature and psychology, but he is very
much alive to the possibility of mistaking hysterical or
hallucinatory phenomena for visions and revelations
whose source is divine. And not only that, but he is prepared to accept the possibility that God may use the natural phenomena of the sense and imagination to achieve
his ends, so that in a given case a vision, for example,
might be the same kind of phenomenon as a hallucination, in other words, a very natural and almost normal
event in psychopathology but used by God as he might
use any other phenomena of the natural order for a purpose of his own.

In the very first page of his preface Father Gabriel
tells us that:

> even in our own day there is too much credulity in
> this department and it is a credulity that leads to de-
> plorable consequences, which are inimical to the real
> progress of the spiritual life,

and just before that he says:

Although the attitude of these mental scientists with respect to such extraordinary graces has become increasingly severe, nevertheless we cannot say that among spiritual persons an attitude of prudence in regard to these matters is as yet general.

The whole purpose of the book, indeed, might be defined as a serious attempt to produce this proper attitude of prudence and to get the whole area of visions and revelations into proper perspective. Karl Rahner also points out that "weakness of faith . . . can drive people to excessive credulity where visions and prophecies are concerned." (Rahner, 1965, p. 89). It is worth noting here that the strict ecclesiastical (as compared very often to the ordinary religious person's) attitude to so-called mystical phenomena has always been one of extreme caution. In Belgium alone in the nineteenth century there were two hundred alleged stigmatists, not one of whom was declared authentic by the Church. Through the centuries only three stigmatists have been recognized authoritatively: St. Francis of Assisi, St. Catherine of Siena, and St. Gemma Galgani. The number of apparitions which has been officially sanctioned (such as that of Lourdes) compared with the number of claims made, again indicates the extreme caution of ecclesiastical authority in this field.

In order to clarify our thinking with regard to these phenomena it is important to recall the psychology of some of the processes of sensation and perception.

2. *Imagery and Associated Phenomena*

In the interaction of organism and environment certain nerve-endings (the peripheral receptors) respond to their adequate and proper stimuli: physical, electromagnetic or chemical as the case may be. The result of this stimulation is the process called sensation. In the intact conscious organism the process of perception supervenes at once on the process of sensation. This means that instead of becoming aware of mere sensory data: colors, sounds, smells, or of the stimulation of the end receptors, we become aware instead of *things*: meanings or meaningful experiences. We "see" tables, chairs, people, oranges and lemons, and not just patches of color of various dimensions. The psychology of perception is vastly complicated both by subjective processes and by external conditions. Always, however, a synthesis of sensory data is effected and memory and imagination play their part. Memory enables us to recall similar phenomena and recognize the present material, while imagination supplements the present fragmentary sensory material with data from the same or other sensory modalities. Intellect, by abstraction from the sensory material, forms concepts, which lead to understanding and generalization. One cannot stress too often the fact that there is no knowledge in the mind other than what has been received through the external senses, molded in perception or abstracted by intellect. There is no other channel through which knowledge of any kind can be naturally attained. The alleged phenomena of telepathy and parapsychology in general would require an extensive treatment on their own. It is enough to say for the moment that there is no such thing as extrasensory perception (with all due respect for the scientific integrity of J. B. Rhine (1935) and his followers). The temptation to think that somehow the mind is equipped naturally with some form of innate knowledge has constantly misled philosophers and others from Plato through Descartes to the archetypal images of the universal unconscious of Jung.

But the fact that there is no innate cognitive content in the human mind and that all its natural knowledge is acquired through sensory experience and the subsequent normal cognitive processes does not mean that supernaturally no other kind of knowledge can be acquired. If God wishes to give a further kind of knowledge to a human being, how can this be done? Man's nature being what it is and God's omnipotence being what it is, the only possibilities (apart from a radical change in human nature itself) are either:

(a) the production of the *effects* of a normal stimulation of the peripheral receptors without an adequate stimulus; or

(b) the production of the sensory synthesis, which would normally be the result of perception without adequate sensory material to work on, *i.e.* the planting of an image in whatever part of the cortex is concerned with forming images; or

(c) the direct production in the intellect of a conceptual content without the process of abstraction from sensory material, *i.e.* the planting of knowledge directly in the intellect.

All three types of "vision" are found in the lives of visionaries and mystics, but the first two are also akin to phenomena found in morbid states of pathological personalities.

When a cognitive content is produced in either of the first two ways it is called in the case of (a) an external vision, and in the case of (b) an imaginary vision.

(a) *An external vision*, regarded strictly as a phenomenon different in mode from the imaginary vision, can be of two kinds. There is nothing to prevent the omnipotence of God from stimulating a peripheral receptor so that the effect will be such as might have been produced by an adequate stimulus. Clearly this will give an "external vision," *i.e.* the cognitive experience of seeing something with no natural cause to account for it. For example, God could create an image on the retina which would produce the same result as an object reflecting light into the eye and producing a retinal image. God could create the retinal image and the individual would think he saw the object. The subject's experience is *as if* he were being stimulated. There would be no way of distinguishing between a retinal image produced miraculously in this way and an object the individual thought he was seeing in the ordinary way, except perhaps by cross-checking on tactile experience like Macbeth and the dagger. "Come, let me clutch thee. I have thee not and yet I see thee still."

The second possible kind of external vision is the production of a sensory object or percept, which then stimulates the receptors in the normal way. In other words, God could create a percept, he could create some physical object, to which we would respond visually. This kind of external vision, however, is very close to the commonplace phenomenon of hallucination. As Father Gabriel points out, both visions of this kind and hallucinations "may be the work of the same psychological mechanism." But he adds, "the cause which sets the mechanism in motion is completely different."

(b) *An imaginary vision*: the term "imaginary vision" is psychologically acceptable but colloquially misleading. "Imaginary" is one of the words referred to at the outset as different in ordinary speech and in technical language. Here it does not mean unreal or fictitious or fabricated, but is simply the adjectival form of the noun *imagination* (the capacity of the mind to re-instate in consciousness the product of sensory stimulation in the absence of an adequate stimulus), and it means simply "the product of imagination." God could plant an image of this kind in the cortex, but its character will be such as might have been produced by a human imagination given the requisite material.

(c) The third possibility as distinct from "external" visions or "imaginary" visions is the implanting of knowledge directly in the intellect. This is infused knowledge and means knowledge given in its final form of conceptual knowledge or judgment directly communicated to the intellect.

These three processes, (a) (b) and (c), if they take place or have taken place, are direct interventions of divine power in the ordinary course of nature, that is, they are miraculous. We cannot rule out the possibility that there may have been interventions of God producing "visions" in any of these three ways.

It is important at this point to consider some of the psychological processes associated with the phenomena of hallucination and imagery, and particularly the phenomenon known as eidetic imagery. An image in the psychological sense is any sensory representation of any kind which emerges in consciousness otherwise than by the stimulation of a peripheral receptor. Normally (in the sense of "for the most part") this kind of sensory representation will be less vivid, less intense, less complete than the immediate result of perception ("the percept"). But this need not be so. There are several kinds of image which can be just as vivid as the percept, sometimes more so. These are still "normal" in the sense that, while they may not be found "for the most part," they are certainly not abnormal phenomena. The *primary memory image* is of this kind, the image we unconsciously carry of the first few words of a sentence while listening to the end. The image of an object in an artist's mind when in the popular phrase he "paints from memory," or which he bears of his model while studying his canvas even when he paints from life, is of this order. But especially the *eidetic image* which is found in about fifty per cent of all children and young adolescents illustrates the point. The child so gifted can look at a complicated pattern (*e.g.* a picture, or a series of small objects) for a space of time too brief to allow the accurate study of even a fraction of the whole, and can then "project" the image on to a neutral ground and read off the details. For the most part this must be done quickly after the stimulation of the receptors. But the image may reappear later at unknown intervals of time. This image is plastic, modifiable, and can assume a vividness of coloring or accurate delineation of line greater than of the original stimulus-pattern. It can be either voluntary or involuntary. If the "ground" is moved, for example through an angle of ninety degrees, the child will turn his head and "follow" the revolving image. This, however, is not hallucination. The child retains complete insight and knows he is not "seeing" an objective picture. In the case of hallucination, insight is the first thing to go, and the individual really believes he is experiencing a transubjective percept. But the point at the moment is simply this: the degree of vividness of an image is not a guarantee of its objectivity.

In the ordinary operation of mind an image does not occur as an isolated phenomenon but as one event in a complicated structure in which emotion, impulse, instinct and desire can all play a part. The emotional tone and motor set of an image are perfectly normal phenomena, in both senses of "normal" mentioned above. The important fact, however, is that while normally an image

arouses an emotion, the causal sequence can readily operate the other way, so that the experience of an emotion
can produce a flood of imagery. The lover, experiencing
a flood of tender emotion, sees the loved one in every
face in a crowd. This is the case also with children who,
on experiencing loneliness or a loss of the sense of security
in the dark, proceed to experience the emotion of fear,
which at once peoples their "imagination" (and the
room) with spectres and ogres. Exactly the same phenomenon takes place in anxiety-states at adult levels (especially in cases of so-called free-floating anxiety), and in
some phases of paranoia and schizophrenia. The process
is the same in the normal and abnormal states; only the
content and the degree of insight into the reality or
transubjectivity of the projected image is different.

If God proceeds by either of the first two methods of
producing images described above, (a) and (b), then the
natural powers of the mind must take over and interpret
the sensory material. Two very important points arise
here:

(1) The first is that in the kind of imagery called a
vision, if the vision is in terms of the created percept
or the retinal image or the image in the cortex, the
intellect has to take over and conceptualize it. This
is the function of the intellect on the natural level..
The result is that the vision is always interpreted in
terms of the receiving personality and the receiving
culture. It is interesting to note that the content of
visions always corresponds to the cultural stereotypes
of the visionary or is closely related to the conven-
tions of creative art, dress, mores, *etc.* in the particular culture.

(2) Furthermore, hallucinations are far more numer-
ous than visions. In almost two thousand years of

Christianity there must have been many cases of schiz-
ophrenics hearing voices, and many of these heard
voices as from the Holy Spirit speaking to them, but
among them are only very few where there is even
a reasonable presumption that the "voices" were from
the Holy Spirit. There are only three possibilities in
fact in phenomena of this kind: they may be divine
or human or diabolical in source. The likelihood of a
diabolical source can be disregarded. The vast majority of these phenomena are wholly natural in source.
They spring from the human psyche, not from God
nor from a diabolical agency.

The notion of the power of Satan:

(1) We do not know the possible upper limit of the
power of a disembodied spirit. But although we do
not know the extent of the power of Satan we do
know that it is a finite power. According to theological principles, a disembodied spirit is never local-
ized in or at a particular place but operates simply
by its own power (*"virtute sua"*).

(2) The idea of the power of Satan raises both a
metaphysical problem and a problem of physical
science. The metaphysical problem is how a dimen-
sionless being outside the laws of space and time could
affect a being or an object which is physically ex-
tended within space and time. The problem of physical science is related to the law of conservation of
energy. If a disembodied spirit acts as a source of
energy, then it will be adding to the total energy in
the material universe.

(3) A third suggestion that has been put forward is
that somehow nonmaterial beings can be a source of

"psychic" energy and that this brings about the requisite changes. The concept of psychic energy was used in respect of the human mind by both Spearman and Freud. According to Spearman (1923) it was a physical quantity directed hither or thither ("mentally or physically") but could not keep up the same pressure in both directions. This is a purely physical concept. Freud's concept of psychic energy was also a material concept.

There cannot be such an entity as "psychic" energy. If it is energy, it is a physical entity. If it is not energy, it cannot affect a physical or material object. A disembodied spirit therefore cannot affect a physical or material object except by miracle *i.e.* a direct intervention by divine power in the ordinary operations of the natural universe. This means that belief in the occurrence of diabolical possession, obsession,[1] and similar so-called "preternatural" manifestations can be ruled out. There can be no obligation to believe in such matters. These phenomena are for the most part related to human psychopathology, or to the credulity of the naive or culturally deprived sectors of humanity.

Natural basis of majority of "visions": There is no reason to expect among holy people a higher percentage of normally balanced minds than throughout the rest of the population. If anything, one might expect, at any rate in some social conditions, a higher percentage of maladjusted people leaning for support on religion. There are then two factors to be reckoned with: a person of un-

---

1. *Obsession* is defined as the continuous presence of the devil to a human being, but in a way that is extrinsic to the person.

Possession is the situation where the diabolical presence is regarded as being intrinsic to the person.

balanced emotional life may, under the stimulus of an emotion, produce an image (in the literal sense) whose content will be that of the kind of imagery most prevalent in his mind, and in the case of a religious person this will most likely be imagery of a religious character. The process of projection can then bring about hallucination. The other possibility is that children and young adolescents whose eidetic imagery is particularly vivid may project on to a neutral background (*e.g.* a dark recess or a cloud) an eidetic image corresponding to a statue or a picture they have seen. It is worth noting that the so-called phenomenon of "photographic memory" is nothing but a carry-over of the gift of eidetic imagery into adulthood. It is not to be wondered at, therefore, that some adults will produce hallucinations of this type. For the sake of clarity it must be stated that the word hallucination is used here, because an eidetic image in which insight into its subjective character is lacking, conforms fully to the psychology of hallucination. Moreover, hallucination does not necessarily mean a morbid state of mental health any more than illusion does.

The content of hallucination, whether auditory or visual, will, like the dream content, always be found to be analyzable into elements of the subject's past experience, since all the content naturally in the mind will have come through the senses. It may, however, be found in bizzare combinations and structures which may make it seem new or novel. The technique of dream analysis, apart from the interpretation of symbolic content, consists simply in tracing the dream-content to its original sensory source. If on occasion a vision (external or "imaginary") or an auditory hallucination can be shown to have a content demonstrably not derivable from the possible sensory experience of the subject (*e.g.* a vision of future events

or an auditory hallucination in a language utterly unknown to the subject), then one has a negative criterion
by which to rule out the human subjective source of the
phenomenon. The decision as to whether a given phenomenon of this order is human or not is best left to the
combined judgment of theologians and psychiatrists. It is
the theologian's task to pronounce on the doctrinal or
moral content and the effects of such a phenomenon, but
the psychiatrist's to decide whether or not the personality
of the subject is such that these phenomena conform to
what in his experience belong to the realm of pathological emotional states. If the moral content is unworthy
of a divine source, or if the doctrine is questionable on
grounds of orthodoxy, the phenomenon is human in
origin. But even if the moral and doctrinal content are
beyond reproach, but the personality is such that phenomena of this kind might be expected, it is again reasonable to postulate a human source. In attempting to evaluate such phenomena there is no point in investigating the
phenomena themselves. There are no special indices attached to guarantee divine origin. The channels of experience are the same for the holy person and for the mentally ill. The only criterion given to us is in terms of the
consequences of the events: *"By their fruits you shall
know them."* In arriving at a judgment about the origin
of the phenomena there are three criteria which must
first be applied:

(a) The type of personality who claims to have had
such experience;
(b) the content of the imagery; and
(c) the effects on the spiritual life and natural mental
health of the individual involved and of the people
associated with him.

The first is important but by no means final. A saint or a sinner can both be chosen for such favors. St. Paul was not a saint on the road to Damascus. The second criterion is also of only limited value. If the moral or spiritual content of the imagery conflicts with faith or morals, then its source cannot be divine. But the fact that the content from this point of view is irreproachable is not of itself a proof of divine origin; it can still be merely human.

The third criterion involves a long-term process, not easily applied in any case, but if something like mass hysteria sets in or if there is evidence of petty lying or deceit, the whole thing can be discounted. It will be seen from this paragraph that there is no easy way of deciding about the origin of these phenomena. For that reason the teaching of St. John of the Cross is very salutary. It can be summed up simply by saying that an individual should take no notice of visions and revelations, but live his spiritual life on a basis of faith, hope and charity. If the alleged visions are divine, God will see to it if he wishes that this becomes abundantly clear. If they are not, then no harm will be done.

Some of the most difficult problems in psychopathology, as well as in the realm of visions and revelations, are presented by the hysterical personality. Hysteria is a form of illness whose manifestations are legion. We shall consider only two forms: hysterical anaesthesia and conversion hysteria. In the former, sensation or sensibility is lost in a strictly limited field without any discernible organic lesion. In the latter, the repressed emotion is converted into a physical symptom. The symptom produced can be almost anything: a pain in the back, laryngitis, coughing, headache, high temperature, insomnia, anaemia, loss of weight, *etc.* But more to our purpose, it can be a visible lesion of the periphery. In the light of this and referring to a famous experiment carried out by Hadfield (1917), it will not be surprising if occasionally alleged stigmatists are found to be hysterical personalities. Dermatology and other medical disciplines and particularly psychosomatic medicine are establishing ever more clearly and definitely the role of emotions in the aetiology of all sorts of disorders.

In hysterical anaesthesia, one is very close to the phenomena of rapture and ecstasy. No case of levitation through hysteria is recorded in the literature so perhaps this phenomenon can be excluded. But trance, catalepsy, loss of sensibility, amnesia, loss of orientation and adaptation to environment, depersonalization, blindness, deafness, insensibility to pain, paralysis, rigidity, all these phenomena and many others of visionaries have their counterpart at least in the phenomena of hysteria.

With regard to conversion symptoms, the connection between hypnosis and hysteria must be borne in mind. Dissociation is charateristic of both phenomena. By this is meant (again in analogical and merely descriptive terms) the fact that a process or content ordinarily under the control of central consciousness is split off, as it were, and maintains a quasi independent existence or functioning of its own.

"Mystical" Phenomena: It is quite possibly true to say that there are no observable phenomena which are entitled to the adjective "mystical." All the phenomena allegedly called mystical are either non-existent or are capable of being reproduced in pathological personalities. Among the most frequently mentioned non-existent phenomena can be listed bilocation, telekinesis, extrasensory perception, clairvoyance and levitation.

Bilocation means the presence in two places at the

same time of the same person, and there are apparently attested cases of it in records of the lives of some saints. This, if it is taken literally, is a metaphysical impossibility. It involves duplication of existence and it is completely unintelligible that even by miracle the human organism should be existing in two distinct places simultaneously. What is perhaps possible is that the person could be in one place and that the experience of seeing him could be produced in another person in another place by some miraculous process. But this is not bilocation. Bilocation proper could not occur even by miracle.

Telekinesis means action at a distance and refers to the possibility of a human agent's affecting the behavior of physical objects without being physically in contact with them and without any instrumental intervention (as in the "spoon-bending" activities of Uri Geller). This is physically impossible. The human mind alone cannot affect the movement of physical bodies.

Extrasensory perception: belief in this is a failure both of reason and faith. It is a failure of reason because if perception means anything it means the reception of a stimulus and the response to it. This means a receptor system capable of receiving the stimulus and responding to it. When we pursue the idea of extrasensory perception or ESP, we find that stimuli unknown to physicists are being received by receptors unknown to physiology. This is an irrational process. It is failure of faith when people pin their faith to this sort of thing as though it were establishing the reality of the spirit and therefore somehow giving us ground for belief in the supernatural. If we need this kind of evidence to reinforce our belief in the reality of the supernatural this is already a failure of faith.

The arguments for ESP are usually based on statistics.

There is an upper limit to chance expectation of correct guessing, so if somebody is guessing, for example, what cards will turn up in the pack and guesses correctly at a much higher level than the limit of chance expectation, this is still not evidence for some extrasensory power. It may merely prove that the human mind is not a random guessing machine.

Clairvoyance: the degree to which people assent to the possibility of clairvoyance or "second sight" is in inverse ratio to their degree of cultural formation. The fundamental principle in all these matters is that natural phenomena have a natural explanation within the ken of the empirical sciences.

Levitation refers to the elevation of the body from the ground and the consequent reversal of the law of gravity. It must be emphasized that miracles do not occur unless there is very grave reason for invoking divine omnipotence.

Reginal Omez (1953) in his book on psychical phenomena is an example of the excessive credulity in this area which is so harmful to genuine faith. He believes in the occurence of telekinesis, levitation, radiesthesia, teleradiesthesia, telepathy, clairvoyance, extrasensory perception, and all the rest of the stock-in-trade of the psychical researcher, parapsychologists and psiphenomenologists, and he still believes it all apparently even after the evidence he himself records of fraud, negative results, inconclusive experiments and unscientific hypotheses.

Ghosts and poltergeists: Most people throughout the world find themselves giving at least a hesitant assent, more often perhaps than a complete belief, to stories about ghosts, poltergeists and such phenomena. It is worth reminding ourselves that we are all a little bit afraid of the point-blank statement: *"There are no such things as ghosts.*" We are afraid of saying this because at the back of our minds there is a carry-over from infancy, a sort of lurking half-formed idea that "there might be something in it." More adult levels of thought perhaps are haunted by the phrase, "There are more things in heaven and earth, Horatio, than are dreamed of in your philosophy." The reluctance people experience to face questions like *"Are there ghosts?"* and answer them with a straight negative is due to the survival within all of us of many infantile, prerational, prescientific frames of reference which color all our thinking.

The cultural anthropologist and the sociologist have a principle which is relevant here: *"If men define situations as real, they are real in their consequences."* (Thomas, 1951). In other words, if you really and truly believe in ghosts or poltergeists (just as if you really and truly believe in other myths: the blood myth or race myth), then although there is nothing behind it, it will have real consequences in your behavior. So we observe throughout the world, through studies of cultural anthropology and social psychology that most cultures have dimensions which are directly the result of belief in the existence of ghosts, poltergeists and preternatural visitors of all kinds. Belief in such things would appear to be a universal human phenomenon but of course belief in a phenomenon no matter how universal does not in any sense establish the reality of the phenomenon believed in. Let us repeat, therefore, it is the consequence of the belief, for example fear, anxiety, placating of the demons that haunt our minds, that are real, but the demons, ghosts and poltergeists are not.

The most prevalent contemporary form of belief in ghosts is the very widespread belief in flying saucers, so-called *Unidentified Flying Objects* of the official reports, and the belief in little green men with pointed heads observing us from other planets. And there are, of course, other contemporary forms of belief in ghosts and poltergeists in our twentieth century folklore, such things as the alleged psychic function of extrasensory perception, clairvoyance, telepathy, telekinesis, to name only a few. Seances and spiritualism, table-rapping, ouija boards, all these testify to the same kind of belief, a belief in witches, ghosts, poltergeists and various kinds of preternatural phenomena. The story of Borley Rectory, one of the best-known stories in recent mythology, was believed absolutely by many, and a book entitled *The Most Haunted House in England* (Price, 1940) simply assumed that the ghosts were there. One could sense the reluctance felt by many to relinquish belief in Borley even when the Borley myth was exploded (Price, 1946). And finally, many people who are otherwise balanced and sane will stake their reputation on such things as water-divining and they get very upset indeed if one casts doubts on so-called water-divining.

If we ask whence comes this universal or near-universal belief in such things, the answer is that we are haunted within ourselves, haunted by factors welling up from the deep unconscious. These are the only real ghosts. Because we experience this anxiety, fear of the unknown, fear of responsibility, fear of the forces of nature and so on, we fall back on the familiar defence-mechanism of projection. We project our fear on to *something,* rather than acknowledge that it is springing up from within ourselves. And what more likely way of getting rid of a fear than to project it on to something which can then be banished, exorcised. We try to drive away the ghost. If we cannot drive away the ghost, if he is still there, then at least we still have sufficient reason to justify our fear to ourselves. We have created a cause for a fear which is there in any case. The mechanism of projection is strictly an infantile process. When the infant through his own clumsiness trips over a chair and falls, he blames the chair, and his mother very often teaches him to do just that. So the short answer to the question *Are there ghosts? Are there poltergeists?* is: There are no ghosts or poltergeists if by this is meant non-material beings which can haunt places or people or things and dispose of physical objects, and perhaps be seen or heard, or their consequences seen or heard: in that sense there are no ghosts or poltergeists. But in the other sense, the psychological sense, it would be rare indeed to find a human mind which was not itself haunted by its own version of ghosts and poltergeists springing up from within itself.

The whole range of alleged phenomena concerning ghosts and poltergeists is simply part of a much wider set of processes: these are survivals throughout our culture and indeed in most cultures that we know of, of very primitive attempts to understand the world around us. Very primitive attempts to understand the world always involve notions of magic and witchcraft, whatever words one uses to describe these phenomena. Sympathetic magic is the attempt to use an object or a person by reason of its relationship or alleged relationship to some other person or thing, to bring about effects in the other person or thing, e.g. sticking pins into a small effigy of a person in order to hurt him. Black and white magic both survive in our countryside. Black magic is the use of practices in themselves ineffective such as the planting of eggs in the foundations of a house in order to do harm to another. White magic is the use of inefficacious means in order to do good to another. We find white magic surviving often in alleged "cures" attached to fairy trees, such as the one on the road to Limerick near Borris, Co. Offaly. We have, of course, sometimes sanctified these primitive survivals from pre-Christian times by giving a saint's name to them. Most people seem to believe in the notion of a "sixth sense" or in some form of clairvoyance. This seems to be particularly true of all the groups of peoples on the "Celtic Fringe" of Europe. But the same idea of a "sixth sense" survives in other cultures in continental Europe itself and probably througout the world.

Pre-christian cults, pre-christian deities, pre-christian religions survive in modified forms and usually we call these things by the generalized name of "witchcraft." Witchcraft is certainly pagan survivals of a pagan religion still active in our midst. And there are much less important survivals of magic and witchcraft in such things as "touch wood" when you hear bad news, or "cross your fingers" or "keep your fingers crossed" in order to achieve some purpose, or you see two people who suddenly say the same thing simultaneously and then hook their little fingers together to annul the magic of having said the same thing simultaneously.

If one asks point-blank *Are there ghosts? Are there poltergeists?* one must distinguish these two questions from *Is man mortal? Does he have a spiritual soul? Will he survive the death of the body?* The answer to the last three questions for the believing Christian of course is *yes.* The answer to the first two, *Are there ghosts? Are there poltergeists?* is *Certainly not,* in the sense in which people believe in ghosts and poltergeists, that is to say, there are not ethereal, milky, shapeless, shimmering bodies called ghosts which actually haunt places, and there are not poltergeists, these alleged playful ghosts or noise ghosts whose function, according to the folklore that surrounds them, is to carry out playful but destructive acts.

Are there ghosts? The answer is *no*. But then how can one prove a negative? Always people appeal to survivals of magical thinking in their attempts to explain that there are ghosts. But they do not recognize that their attempts to explain ghosts are survivals of magical thinking. For example, most people who talk about extrasensory perception, clairvoyance, telepathy and so on, appeal to unknown stimuli received by unknown receptors for the alleged transference of knowledge from one mind to another, and this of course is magical thinking. A good deal of what was thought in former times to be evidence for the existence of ghosts and poltergeists is now brought successfully under the twin heads of hypnosis and depth psychology.

There are many other forms of the survival of the irrational in our midst: prejudices between one group and another, personifications of disease, personification of evil or of chance or of luck. One is familiar with the phrases throughout the countryside, *Good luck* or *As luck would have it,* or *His luck left him* or *He had no luck* with, for example, the purchase of a calf or a cow or something. These personifications of chance or luck, of evil or disease, are part of the survival of the irrational or primitive or pre-christian religion. But there are other forms of irrational survivals. In America, for example, there are people who apparently still believe that the earth is flat, there is the survival of Druid rituals in Wales, and the re-emergence of a whole new witchcraft lore in England and indeed in Ireland, all these indicate that we are very far removed from the rational creatures we would like to be.

Perhaps the most important thing to be said at this point is that through our understanding of hypnosis and depth psychology and the survivals of the irrational in our midst we can now give a perfectly valid account of many phenomena which in the past were thought to be "mystical phenomena." We can bring them now under the general head of "psychopathology," in other words evidence of a disturbed personality rather than of great holiness.

To the question *Are there poltergeists?* the answer is that the very notion of poltergeist is quite a new addition to the folklore of the cultures to which we belong. It dates from about the 16th century in Germany but only from about the early 19th century in Britain and Ireland. The theory is that poltergeists are playful ghosts. Thurstone (1953) thought that they were the souls of unbaptized children who died before they could grow sufficiently to have their childish fun, so the ghosts of these children are now having their fun by throwing furniture around and making noise and doing all the usual things attributed to poltergeists. The accounts given of the alleged activities of poltergeists are very similar wherever they occur. The usual phenomena involve such things as butter on the ceiling and broken eggs on the floor, furniture turned upside down, noise of rattling stones and other irrational events calculated perhaps more to frighten than to destroy. It is worth looking at these alleged accounts of phenomena pretty closely and asking the question: *How could the physical events described or alleged to have occurred actually occur?* If the alleged cause, the poltergeist, is in fact tossing things around, interfering with physical things in any way, then this raises two insoluble difficulties. One is that the alleged ghost is a nonmaterial being and could not in fact therefore throw stones or upset furniture because he could not interact with physical things. The second difficulty is that he would be disposing of physical energy without a physical source for the energy: in other words, he would be adding to the total amount of energy in the universe and this would be a breach of the law of the conservation of energy. If there is no physical source of movement there must be a nonphysical source and therefore an addition to the amount of energy in the universe, which is impossible. The only alternative to these impossibilities, *i.e.* the impossibility of the ghost interfering with physical things or adding to the physical energy in the world, is the postulating of endless miracles. One could indeed envisage a situation whereby the ordinary physical laws of space-time could be suspended. But then we must remember that a miracle requires divine intervention and divine intervention will never be on the flimsy, irrational, infantile, purposeless, silly kind of basis attributed to the poltergeist, nor would divine omnipotence ever intervene to carry out the same meaningless acts attributed to poltergeists. For miraculous intervention in the space-time laws, one must have an adequate reason, for example, the good of mankind, and various other factors before one could even begin to postulate divine intervention. There is no adequate reason, no worthy purpose in the alleged phenomenon of poltergeists and it is not for the good of mankind that furniture should be upset. So we can rule out poltergeists and miracle as the explanation of the alleged phenomena.

What then can we say about the alleged phenomena? First of all there is a curious similarity throughout the world between these phenomena wherever they occur. One always finds a family constellation consisting usually of believing, weak, possibly even vacillating parents, a schizoid personality among the children, infants born pretty close together in time and generating between them considerable hostility towards each other, very often "guilt feelings" (not real guilt for any responsible act) haunting the parents, who usually have inadequate personalities, and the whole will be laden with credulity and evidence of other disturbance besides the poltergeist phenomena. Secondly, one finds that the whole picture is an irrational one, and thirdly one finds that the phenomena disappear with the spread of understanding, very often with a little psychotherapy and a little psychological help.

It is often thought that there is some link between the acceptance of such phenomena as ghosts and poltergeists on the one hand and the faith on the other, so that it is sometimes thought that there is a loss or lack of faith involved in the rejection or the denial of the possibility of such phenomena. In fact, not only is there no loss of faith here but the other way around: that is to say that the more we can be rational about these alleged preternatural phenomena and understand their irrational source and be courageous enough to reject all stories alleging the occurence of such events, the more we can do all that, the more purified does our faith become and the more valuable. Because then our choice of an assent of faith is a strictly supernatural assent on the basis of revelation, not on the basis of alleged experience of these so-called preternatural events. It is also true and it should be added here that wherever investigations have been carried out, with very few exceptions, natural explanations have been found for the alleged phenomena, and where natural explanations are not yet available it is because due to the fallibility of human testimony the alleged events could not be verified. Individuals who have claimed clairvoyance and telepathy, for example the famous Pilkingtons, subsequently explained that their clairvoyance was a stage trick, a coded message system in which no clairvoyance was involved. There remains a residual set of phenomena, for example in the records of the *Society for Psychical Research,* for which neither natural explanation nor trickery can so far be discovered. This does not mean that we have to fall back on preternatural explanations. It may very well be that the phenomena which have not been explained did not in fact occur, and those which did occur will eventually be found to have a natural explanation.

CHAPTER V

CONVERSION

In his classic work, A Grammar of Assent, Cardinal Newman (1870) is concerned with the nature and problems of belief:

> In religious inquiry each of us can speak only for himself, and for himself he has a right to speak. His own experiences are enough for himself, but he cannot speak for others: he cannot lay down the law; he can only bring his own experience to the common stock of psychological facts. (1917 impression, pp. 384-385)

Cardinal Newman, with great insight and foresight, saw that the psychology of natural human processes must be at the base of what he calls "assent in religion." Each man must state what he "holds to be sufficient." This however is not to make the assent of faith a purely subjective matter, even though it must always be the free act of choice of an individual subject. It is rather to emphasize the fact that the occasion, the stimulus, the precipitating factor or factors which bring about the act of faith (conversion to the faith), or disbelief (the abandonment of the faith) can be found in almost any human experience.

There are no specific psychological processes discernible in conversion to the faith which are not found in any or all other changes in values, attitudes and beliefs, *i.e.* there is no specific 'psychology of conversion.' 'Conversion' here defined to mean the embracing in faith of the truth of the Revelation of Christ, takes place on the human plane through the normal human resources of weighing evidence, assessing values, placing trust or withholding it, eliminating prejudices, stereotypes, irrational or unreasonable attitudes, abandoning inadequate value systems, etc., all as seen through the eyes of the prospective convert.

In his account of conversion, Chapters IX and X of The Varieties of Religious Experience, William James (1902) makes many important comments, among which from our point of view the two most important are (1) the theory that conversion can and does occur as a "piece of natural psychology," and (2) that the alleged "non-natural" or "super-normal" incidents of sudden conversions "may all come by way of nature, or worse still, be counterfeited by Satan." (p. 236)

While it will be argued here that conversion to the faith as we understand it is not simply "a piece of natural psychology," never the less the truth of James' theory and of Cardinal Newman's statement just quoted lies in the old theological concepts of God's grace working in us *humano modo,* (in a human way, or through the natural processes of the human psyche), and secondly, in the maxim *omne quod recipitur ad modum recipientis recipitur* (whatever is received is received after the manner of the recipient). What this concept means in the context of phenomena of conversion is this: all the "phenomena" of conversion will be describable events in the behavior and the mental processes of the convert. James is quite right in thinking that the phenomena are not themselves the conversion, since, as we have seen, these can be the result of natural psychology, or indeed simulated in various ways. It must be stressed that factors on the purely human empirical plane do not themselves explain "belief in things unseen," *i.e.* supernatural faith. They simply name some of the mechanisms on the natural plane whereby faith is achieved. As we have seen elsewhere "Flesh and blood" do not reveal the truths of Christ, "but my Father who is in heaven." (Mt 16:17)

It is not suggested, nor must one read into the above, any suggestion that the truths of faith are or can be evidenced by sensory experiences. We use the word "evidence" in a very special sense to mean the "cumulation of probabilities which psychologically bring about the assent." (Newman, *op. cit.*) One must remember however that rational arguments alone do not of themselves produce supernatural faith. *"Non in dialectica complacuit Deo salvum facere populum suum"* (St. Ambrose).

Other authors, especially more recent ones, are not as cautious or as clear-sighted as William James' pioneering work shows him to have been. Thus, for example, we find that some authors equate different forms of subjectively recorded experiences as though they were identical and equally valid, simply because the phenomena of the experiences as subjectively reported appear to be composed of the same type of psychological events. We have already noted in Chapter I the fallacy of psychomechanistic parallelism as formulated by Gregory Zilboorg. (cf. Braceland, 1955, p. 111) In the context of conversion, the fallacy consists in arguing that because some emotional experiences or "illuminations" or sense of the "conviction of sin," or the relief of "being saved," or indeed any other overwhelming psychological events can and do occur, and are described as occurring in different contexts, therefore the experiences are coordinate and in some sense identical, whether they be called conversion, ecstasy or mystical phenomena. Our argument about the mystical (pp. 58ff. and 87ff. above) applies substantially also to the notions of conversion and ecstasy. Subjectively reported experiences are not a guarantee of their origin or of their validity. One must therefore once again make the point that it is not the observable experience in itself, but the innermost nature of the experience, and the frame of reference through which it is interpreted that are important:

> God is hidden behind the veil of secondary causes as far as His ordinary presence and action in Nature are concerned. He hides His supernatural action and presence of love in the soul of the just behind the veil of faith. . . . (Louismet, 1924, p.1)

One encounters the same fallacy in Huxley's *Doors of Perception,* Sargant's *Battle for the Mind,* and most recently perhaps in a G. A. P. publication: *Mysticism: Spiritual Quest or Psychic Disorder* (1976).

Huxley (1961) taught that so-called preternatural experience, whether produced by drugs or otherwise, is equated with specifically religious experience. As Zaehner (1957) puts it, Huxley "implies unmistakably that what he experienced after taking mescalin was explicable in terms of 'contemplation at its height.'" William Sargant (1957) showed that the observed physiological phenomena were much the same in various forms of political and religious conversion, and could be brought about by various processes such as those observed in psychopharmacology, psychotherapy, conditioning and "brainwashing." The processes involved are not really comparable to conversion in spite of what Sargant says. Thus Lifton (1957) says:

> It is quite clear that thought reform (brainwashing) resembles, in many features, *an induced religious conversion*, as well as *a coercive form of psychotherapy*. These comparisons can be made profitably, but should not be put forth loosely. There remain important differences among these various approaches to 'changing' the individual personality. (G. A. P., p. 249)

Perhaps the real difference between what happens in "brainwashing" and what happens in other circumstances is describable in terms of Newman's distinction of notional and real assent. Notional assent can be given to a proposition not known to be true, but assented to on grounds other than evidence, while real assent is brought about by evidence based on real understanding. Thus notional assent can be given to a proposition on grounds of its origin, prestige, pragmatic value, or shame producing efficacy, and perhaps in principle even on Pavlovian grounds (reiteration, etc.) but real assent can only be given if the proposition is properly understood and the evidence for it seen to be cogent, and this is clearly missing from any Pavlovian conditioning process.

Clearly one must look behind the phenomena of "conversion" to discern whether there is any reason to accept the possibility of the supernatural action of God and the operation of grace and faith. Precisely because the phenomena (emotional enthusiasm, "illumination," consolation, desolation, etc.) do not of themselves carry with them any supernatural authentication, they cannot of themselves be either the criterion for or the evidence for spiritual renewal or conversion to supernatural faith. It is possible to observe what are sometimes called "conversions" occurring as a result of the pressures of emotion in mass rallies, and in smaller emotionally-charged "religious" meetings of a revivalist or charismatic kind. In these cases, two points should be noted: one is the ephemeral nature of the so-called conversion; the other, perhaps commoner aspect, is the manner in which the emotional experience itself becomes a gratifying and self-rewarding experience. It is of course possible that an overwhelming emotional experience or the social psychological pressures of the group may indeed be the occasion of a genuine conversion, but one must never lose sight of the fact that they themselves are not the conversion proper.

Just as we have seen in a former chapter that grace is not experiencable, and as such is not an efficient cause bringing about changes in the natural order, so we must say that faith (the infused virtue of faith which makes the assent of supernatural faith possible) is not itself a psychological event as cause in the natural order bringing about discernible consequences. It is a supernatural gift which operates more as a formal factor than as an efficient cause, altering the substance of psychological events by supernaturalizing their nature and efficacy, but without changing their observable dimensions in the temporal order. *How* these events take place, *what* brings them about, are important questions, but are irrelevant to their intrinsic nature. It is not the efficient cause that we look to, but the consequences of these events. The only criterion given us in scripture is: "By their fruits ye shall know them." The conversion of St. Augustine, as he describes it himself, may indeed have been the result of his experience of hearing the words: *"Tolle lege"*[1] but the *"Tolle lege"* did not as cause bring about his assent of faith, rather they were the occasion of his eliciting

---

1. Trans. "Take and read."

the act of faith. Here we meet an important distinction in relation to grace and in relation to faith. In relation to grace, the familiar distinction is that between actual and sanctifying grace. "Sanctifying grace" refers to our participation in the Divine life, while actual graces operate as motivations affecting the operation of the will, and the whole personality. Sanctifying grace changes our very mode of existence to make us children of God and heirs, while actual grace operates to affect our modes of behavior. Some actual graces operate as efficacious motivations within the individual to stimulate him to action, *e.g.* feelings, emotions, desires and cognitive factors. Others operate as stimuli or as goals from without, eliciting from outside the personality the response of the individual. Many of these, of course, can be seen as events in the natural order, for example, an encounter between one individual and another, the casual reading of a text or hearing a sermon. But these events may also be seen through the supernatural frame of reference as providential, as indeed they are. As events in space-time, they are accountable for in the order of the space-time continuum. As providential they are seen as actual graces. Once again the choice is between a purely temporal frame of reference and a dual frame of reference as indicated in Chapter III. Using the dual frame of reference, the same set of events can be accounted for in the space-time order, and simultaneously seen in the theological context of providence and the history of salvation. This point of view is in accord with contemporary biblical scholarship which sees the history of Israel as a sequence of events in space-time with their own explanatory causes, while simultaneously reading that history not in theocratic terms, (*viz.* God intervening as first cause in time) but in a theological frame of reference which in fact makes the natural history the history of God's salvific relationship to man.

In considering the nature of conversion, it is important to note that in addition to conversion to the faith one must also note the phenomena of conversion from an immature, inchoate, informal or implicit faith to mature explicit adult commitment. Perhaps we have failed to understand the nature of the transition that occurs very often in adolescence from the immature type of faith of the child to the more explicit faith of the adult. The transition can be marked by severe emotional anguish, even the experience of doubt and questioning, often misunderstood both by the young person himself and by those trying to deal with him. It is of course not suggested here that every adolescent, or even most adolescents go through crises of faith. Rather the point here is that *if* an adolescent experiences what he might think of as doubting or calling in question his faith, this may be the signal for the beginning of genuine adult supernatural faith. His apparent doubting can often be interpreted as the difference between scientifically evidenced knowledge which is his experience in most other dimensions of his intellectual life on the one hand, and the true nature of the voluntary choice of commitment to things unseen which cannot be evidenced by the canons of scientific knowledge on the other. It is here above all that one sees the true nature of conversion, *i.e.* the voluntary conscious choice of commitment to a value system which may change one's life, and to a personal faith which certainly should do so. This can and does occur most often without the internal emotional experiences described by some authors as if they were of the essence of conversion. As Zilboorg points out (in Braceland, 1955, pp. 110-111) St. Thomas Aquinas grounded his concept of faith in reason and intelligence, just as St. John of the Cross taught that "the deep mysticism and contemplation of the mystics . . . had to be based on reason, intellect and rational knowledge."

Described in the spatio-temporal order of psychological experience, "conversion" means a change in a person's attitudes, values, loyalty systems, beliefs and social groupings. To take only a few examples, men have been "converted" from Christianity to Buddhism, from Catholicism to Protestantism, from democracy to Marxism, from liberalism to conservatism; in short, from any one belief-system to another. Moreover, it has been shown that such radical changes of belief systems can sometimes occur through psychotherapy, psychopharmacology, desocialization and loss of identity (cf. Lifton, 1957). Similar changes have been brought about by force and fear, *i.e.* by aggression, punitive measures and torture. There are obvious similarities between these processes and conversion to the faith, but of course there are major differences. In the first place, one must remember that changes of belief, of value systems and of life style can and do occur through the knowledge and the voluntary choices of individuals to commit themselves in the light of knowledge to chosen values. The element of free and voluntary choice is intrinsic to the concept of the act of faith in religious conversion. For this reason alone, apart from any other consideration, one must be hesitant about accepting the highly emotional type of "conversion" occurring in circumstances suggestive of mass hysteria. Once again we must remind ourselves that the precipitating factor which may bring about such a cognitive and volitional change may indeed be the experience of conditioning, social pressures, desocialization, brutality, the experience of impressive or attractive personalities, or almost any other spatiotemporal event. Such precipitating factors are only the occasion, not the cause, of genuine religious conversion. If in fact they are the *cause*, as they might be with some personalities, *e.g.* highly suggestible ones, one should remain sceptical about the reality of the conversion. In the case of "conversions" occurring in what might for some be extremely emotional circumstances, *e.g.* the snake cults of some unhappy forms of Christianity, the *"enthusiasm"* aroused by evangelical mass rallies, or highly charged charismatic meetings, one must not accept too readily a supernatural dimension. Such a dimension *may* indeed be present, but if it is, it will be attested not by the subjective claims of the convert, nor by the approval of those who bring about the conversion, but rather by the long range life style and ultimate eternal destiny of the persons concerned. Genuine supernatural choices of commitment are made under the influence of grace by individuals knowing what they are doing and choosing to do it.

The greatest danger in current theories of the psychology of religion is the over-emphasis on non-rational, emotional factors, together with a sometimes anti-intellectual stance. The danger lies in the fact that the experiences are neither self-validating nor universal. If we teach that they are either self-validating or universal, then those who do not have them (and these are perhaps the majority of people) will be tempted to disclaim any sense of conversion, of faith, or of both, on the grounds of never having experienced such events.

CHAPTER VI

PERSONALITY AND IMMORTALITY

Bertrand Russell several years ago in an article on the possibility of survival after death (*Sunday Times,* January 6, 1957) appealed to Hume. He quoted with evident approval the well known passage in Part IV, Section VI of the *Treatise of Human Nature.* The passage runs:

> For my part, when I enter most intimately into what I call myself, I always stumble on some particular perception or other, of heat or cold, love or hatred, pain or pleasure. I never can catch myself at any time without a perception and never can observe anything but the perception.

What Russell did not explain, and probably could not be expected to explain within the confines of Sunday journalism, was the point at issue in this passage and the premises assumed by Hume which determined his outlook not on this problem alone, but on all philosophical issues. The point at issue is given by Hume in the opening words on the section:

> There are some philosophers who imagine we are every moment intimately conscious of what we call our self: that we feel its existence and its continuance in existence; and are certain beyond the evidence of

a demonstration both of its perfect identity and simplicity.

Hume had in mind the Cartesians and particularly Descartes himself. And there is no doubt that Hume in the passage quoted is right. We do not find a direct awareness of self in any introspectible act of consciousness.

This sometimes strikes people as odd because they have long thought that they had a direct awareness of themselves. St. Thomas argued that a direct awareness of oneself of this kind is the prerogative of the Divine Intellect, whereas our human intellect is aware of itself only through conceptual constructions formed in the same way as we form them about anything else. And this means forming them by intellectual processes whereby we use the data of sense to achieve non sensory intellectual contents. Of what then are we directly aware? Always of some act or content of consciousness: in Hume's terminology, we are aware of some perception of heat or cold, light or shade, love or hatred, etc. But Hume had already ruled out the possibility of there being any mental content other than sensory (and Russell knew this). Hume was well versed in the thought of Berkeley, who had recently ("of late years" is Hume's phrase) denied that there were or could be any such things as abstract ideas. Hume claims this denial of Berkeley's as "one of the greatest and most valuable discoveries. . . ."

It is not difficult in the light of the foregoing paragraph to translate the passage quoted approvingly by Russell from Hume's private language into contemporary English. It would then read: "My introspective knowledge of myself does not reveal anything corresponding to the Cartesian self. I cannot discover any abstract ideas as these are normally understood ('according to the common method of explaining them'—Part 1, Sec. VII. Does this mean a denial of Cartesian innate ideas? If so, Hume is right to that extent). All I can ever discover is a sensory content."

It is unlikely that anyone would quarrel with Hume's denial of the Cartesian self or the Cartesian "clear and distinct ideas," including the idea of "self." But there are many who would question the last assertion: that all I can ever discover is a sensory content. The evidence of experiment is that there exist "contents of consciousness" which are not sensory in character. Few psychologists would now make the claim of Hume, and this for two reasons. First, because of the experimental evidence in regard to consciousness; and second, because of the increased understanding of the unconscious. Hume could not introspect the unconscious, nor can anybody else, and yet it would be rash to deny its existence, its contents and its functions. But there is no reference to these matters in Russell's article. We shall return to the point in a moment in considering the notion of memory and the sweeping assertion of Russell "that the most essential thing in the continuity of a person is memory."

Russell claims to examine the belief in survival "from a purely scientific point of view." This seems to have impressed many readers. The purely scientific point of view means presumably the point of view which claims that (a) it is going to study only observable phenomena, (b) by the methods of observation and experiment. From this point of view it is unscientific to ignore, as Russell does, the experimental and clinical evidence about mind. Moreover, the scientific point of view means the adoption of a methodology which at once rules out the possibility of studying certain kinds of problems: the nature of beauty or moral goodness, for example. And if there are disembodied spirits or angels they will be forever by definition beyond the range of study from the "purely scientific point of view" simply because, not being material in any way, they will not be "observable phenomena." But the fact that something is unobservable does not mean that it does not exist. If one accepts the proposition "that whatever is not observable sensorialy does not exist," then of course the conclusion will follow. But the proposition that "whatever is not observable sensorially does not exist" is not only not known to be true but could not be shown to be true. In other words, it is not a scientific proposition but a dogmatic assumption. Yet it is assumed by Hume and also by Russell.

But Russell's argument depends on his doctrine about memory. "The most essential thing," he tells us, "in the continuity of a person is memory." This has a specious plausibility. It will be true if I state it as follows: "The most essential thing in the awareness of continuity of a person is memory." But this is a radically different proposition. It means, for example, that a person suffering from total amnesia will not be aware of his continuity as a person—he will have "forgotten who he was." This is not at all an impossibility—it happens frequently enough. Yet no one, not even Russell I think, would deny that in total amnesia the patient is still, in a perfectly intelligible sense, the same person that he was before his loss of memory. But in terms of Russell's formulation this would not be so. *The awareness of continuity as a person* is not at all the same thing, logically or psychologically, as *continuity as a person*. Russell concludes: "We may therefore take memory as what defines the continuity of a person." The 'therefore' is good, as it suggests that something has been proved.

The argument from memory, however, can be shown

by a simple tour de force to establish a conclusion which flatly contradicts Russell's conclusion. The argument would take the following form: I can remember something which happened to me twenty years ago. (This would hardly be denied, even by Russell). But if this be so, then I must have had a continuous existence since the event I claim to remember happened. But it cannot be the organism alone which is responsible for this continuous existence, since biologists tell me that all the cells of my organism are different from those which constituted me twenty years ago. Therefore "I" am somehow a persistent entity, even though the organism is constantly changing. But Russell rejects this persistent entity. It will be helpful to consider this a while longer.

The argument is Hume's and runs as follows: "I venture to affirm of the rest of mankind that they are nothing but a bundle or collection of different perceptions which succeed each other with an inconceivable rapidity and are in a perpetual flux or movement. . . . The mind is a kind of theatre where several perceptions make their appearance; pass, repass; glide away and mingle in an infinite variety of postures and situations. . . . ." But he warns us that "the comparison of the theatre must not mislead us": there is really no stage nor any theatre at all, only the succession of scenes. There is no "mind" or "self" but only the succession of mental contents. Hume makes due allowance for anyone "who has a different notion" and says: "All I can allow him is that he may be in the right as well as I"; but Russell makes no such concession. He gives the impression indeed that what he says is scientifically established. Now with regard to Hume's argument, if we speak in terms of the pure experience of consciousness, he is right. That is to say, that as far as experience goes the literal account of mind must be of a series of mental states or contents or processes. But it was long ago pointed out by Bradley that Hume's conception of mind was incomplete in his famous metaphor of mind as a hank of mutually sustaining onions on a non-existent rope. And many philosophers pointed out the philosophical problem which this conception posed but did not answer. If the mind is simply the succession of its own states, then how can it become conscious of itself as a succession of states? For all earlier states have ceased to exist before this present state of mind. The series does not exist but only the momentary term in the series. And it is not profitable to appeal to memory; since by definition mind is only the succession of its states, it must be the present state which remembers all the others. But the present state is by definition only a mental event or content. How can one mental event or content be said to "know" or "remember" another? much less to remember a whole series? And at the same time to account for consciousness and self-consciousness?

Philosophers, like other men, have minds. They are subject to some at least of the defence-mechanisms revealed in analysis: repression, dissociation; perhaps more than any other they are subject to rationalization. John Stuart Mill understood this argument of Hume's and the difficulty of a series becoming conscious of itself as a series. But at least he faced the issue squarely as a scientist should. It was self-contradictory, he thought, that a series should thus become conscious of itself, but he preferred to accept the contradiction rather than the consequence: a substantial persistent entity through time. For this would at once pose the question about the nature of this substantial persistent entity. It is unlikely that Russell was unaware of this problem. But many of his readers would not have heard of it, while scientific integrity would seem to demand that it should have been made clear to them.

Russell goes on: "The question whether we survive death thus becomes the question: Are there, after a man dies, memories of what happened to him while he lived on earth?" It is perhaps trivial to point out the inconsequential "thus" in this sentence. But it is more to the point to examine the question itself. The question presumably does not mean: Does anybody remember what happened to so-and-so while he lived on earth? for this question can certainly be answered in the affirmative without prejudice to any question about survival. The question therefore must mean something else. It might mean: After a man dies, does he remember what happened to him while he lived on earth? But this is no advance over the question: Does man survive death (except perhaps in this sense that survival might be possible without self-consciousness and therefore without memory, as would appear to be the Buddhist view; but this possibility is ruled out in advance for Russell because of his identification of personality with memory). The question thus becomes: Do disembodied memories occur as a series through time?

The apparent simplicity of this question is deceptive. It might mean: Do disembodied memories occur through time with nobody who has these memories? Or it might mean: Do disembodied memories occur through time with nobody who is these memories? The first form of the question does not arise for Russell, since in any case there is nobody who has memories; memories are the person who thinks he has them. This is clear from paragraph 2 of his article: "A critical enquiry does not reveal the existence of any such persistent entity as the core of the personality," where the words "persistent entity" refer to "soul," mind," "self" or "subject." The second form of the question is more important. If disembodied memories occur through time, even though nobody has these memories, they would automatically constitute a person on Russell's premises. Russell's task, therefore, seems a simple one. He has only to show that there are not memories in order to show that there is no survival after death. Up to this point he seems to be using the word "memories" in an ordinary "public" sense to refer to mental events and contents. In any reasonable public use of language one would reason as follows: Memories are either composed of matter or they are not so composed. They are either self-supporting or they are not self-supporting. Russell agrees (par. 9) that "thoughts and feelings are evanescent," and it is precisely on this ground that philosophers argue that these are not self-supporting but demand a subject. In order to avoid this conclusion Russell falls back on the assertion that thoughts and feelings "compose the brain." As the brain is clearly material by any definition it would seem to follow that thoughts and feelings (of which memories are a species) will have to be material. But at this point the argument reverts to a private language: "When I mention the brain in this connection I shall expect to be accused of materialism. This accusation, however, would be unjust." But it is extremely difficult to see how in the usage of any public language this is not materialism. In fact the identification of thought and feelings with the brain is only a surreptitious way of reintroducing the notion of "self" or "subject" but in materialistic terms.

Russell was one of the ablest thinkers of the century and one of the five or six greatest logicians of all time. From the purely scientific point of view, he is open to the criticism that he has not taken account of all the evidence. From the logical point of view he has attempted to establish a universal negative proposition, which notoriously can only be done by deduction from another universal negative. And the one universal negative on which Russell's argument depends ("whatever is not experienced by the senses does not exist") cannot be established.

From the psychological point of view Russell's argument amounts to saying that people believe in survival because of their fears and their wishes. Even if fears or wishes accounted for belief in survival, as they might very well do for many people, the question of survival itself remains to be answered. This is the fallacy of historicism: the fallacy of thinking that because we can explain historically why a particular belief is held, therefore the content of the belief is false. Freud committed this fallacy in connection with the existence of God, and there are many other examples of it, particularly in anthropology, comparative religion, higher criticism and sociology.

Philosophically Russell's article is a good example of finding reasons for a belief held independently of the reasons given for it, in other words it is an example of rationalization.

The argument for survival is extremely complex and in a summary exposition could certainly be unconvincing. Scotus in fact characterized all rational arguments for immortality as merely probable and fell back on faith. But St. Thomas thought it could be proved. The argument depends on (a) the relation between action and agent, (b) the nature of the soul, (c) the relation between matter and spirit, leading to the notion of possibility of survival. From possibility to actual survival the argument takes two steps: one consists in showing that the soul does not by natural means cease to be; the other, in showing that God does not annihilate it. The question of resurrection and bodily survival should not be confused with the question of survival. Resurrection and bodily survival are matters of revealed faith. But the possibility and the fact of immortality, though difficult, are matters that reason can deal with.

It is fairly obvious that if there is no such thing as "soul" there can be no such thing as immortality. One could still argue and reason about the "eternity" of matter but the eternity of matter, either backwards or forwards in time, is irrelevant to the question: do I survive the death of the body?

The problem of the eternity of the world, in so far as reason can cope with it, can be put very simply. Since God always is in an eternal present, the act of creation of a finite universe (speaking anthropomorphically) could have occurred at any "point" in God's existence or could have been "coterminous" with the existence of God. The fact that this was the case is not known from reason but from revelation. The possibility of eternity "forwards" in time follows from the difference between transformation and annihilation of matter. Transformations of matter are familiar. Hydrogen and oxygen "become" or are "changed into" water. There is a loss of energy but it is not simply reduced to nothingness. The energy is taken up by something else.

The notion of nothingness is difficult. It is not just a blank surrounded by something else, as one might think when considering the possibility of a perfect vacuum. There is no known instance of "reduction to nothingness" in the physical world, any more than there is of creation. But the loose and inaccurate use of the word "annihilation" in connection with atomic energy has led people to think that matter is literally "annihilated" or reduced to nothingness. In fact it is converted into energy, and energy is still a phenomenon of the physical material world. The loose use of "annihilation" is parallelled by the equally loose use of the word "creation," as in "steady-state" cosmologies. The "big bang" theory postulates one creative act in the beginning, while "steady-state" theory would seem to contravene the principle of the conservation of energy by postulating the eternal creation of new matter.

There is no known instance of annihilation (in the literal sense) in the physical universe. Appeals to thermodynamics will not help; entropy may mean the cessation of all movement and change but it is not the same as "ceasing to be." Nor does it help to speculate on the possibility of a bomb superior to the hydrogen bomb, of such power, or instigating a chain reaction of such magnitude, that our universe would be "annihilated." For, once again, the position is that our universe would be converted into something else: energy, perhaps, but that can be left to the physicists. Such an event might be the end of "our world" but not necessarily the end of "the world." We must take it that as far as human reason can penetrate the problem, matter could be eternal. Annihilation is the prerogative of divine power, the correlative of creation.

If it is assumed, as Russell seems to assume, that man is nothing but matter, then his "eternity" will follow from the eternity of matter itself. But of course Russell would agree that his continuity as a person would cease. The continuing in existence of the atoms or particles of which I am composed is not at all the same as *my* continuing in existence. It seems that if Russell wished to be completely consistent his argument could have been stated in a few sentences: "I am nothing but a collection of elementary particles organized in a particular way. It is manifest that this organization breaks down. But the particles go on existing. This is not immortality." But the concepts of *me, ego, self, person,* are hard to get rid of. Consciousness and mental life are equally difficult to get rid of. Hence the inevitable falling back on a discussion of memory and continuity rather than a straight statement of the materialist hypothesis.

The "reduction" of man to a group of elementary particles, or more generally, the elimination of any difference between living and nonliving matter has become a habitual mode of thought with many. Sherrington (1951), though he does not subscribe to this doctrine, states it very well. Referring to a well-known passage where Eddington speaks of his table and of his elbow resting on it, Sherrington says:

> True, there is between the elbow and the table the difference that the one is "living" and the other is dead. Chemistry and physics say nothing of this. Or rather, they say a great deal about it but do not in saying it make use of either of these words. If we tell them that the table was at one time living wood and is now dead wood, that the wood was at one time part of a living tree, they do not recognize the word as conveying any radical distinction between the two . . . Chemistry says that neither in the one case nor in the other does it find anything or any behavior which is not chemical. (p. 234).

And again Pirenne (1951) makes an important point:

> An examination of physics qua physics gives no indication that the new physical laws should not apply to the components of the human body.

But neither does Pirenne accept the materialist hypothesis. It would be interesting but perhaps unprofitable to compile a list of quotations from Eddington, Einstein, Hinshelwood, Adrian, each of whom in his own way states the problem and rejects the materialist hypothesis, very often, as with Sherrington, by doing violence to his own scientific thinking. Sherrington is prepared to accept the theoretically impossible, as he puts it, that is to say, he accepts the physicochemical account of man, the reality of mind, the impossibility that mind and matter should affect one another, but accepts in addition that in fact they do so. This would appear to be the position of many others, a sort of reversion to an Averroist "double-truth" theory.

The way out of the apparent impasse depends on hard philosophical thinking. The impasse derives from what Ryle (1949, p. 23) has called the "Official Doctrine," "Descartes' Myth," "the dogma of the Ghost in the Machine." This myth he derives not only from Descartes but also from "Scholastic and Reformation Theology," "Stoic-Augustinian theories of the will," "Platonic and Aristotelian theories of the intellect." In his reasoning he reverts to what is in essence (though not in detail or in the consequences he draws from it) the thomistic concept of man as one being. St. Thomas' problem was not: how is soul as spirit related to a body existing in its own right so that the product is man? This was Plato, St. Augustine, Scotus and Descartes, but rather: given that this being, sitting or standing in front of me, is Socrates, how is it that the following propositions can all be true about him at the same time: he weighs 180 lbs, he is subject to the law of gravity, he grows, he sees, he feels, he thinks? In philosophical terms this is the problem: how is it that one and the same being can sustain apparently contradictory predicates, he is matter, he is spirit?

The solution of Plato and the others listed above consisted always in saying there is no contradiction; he is really two beings and some of these predicates are true of one of these beings and the others are true of the other. But St. Thomas will have none of this. Perhaps his greatest, but certainly his most controversial contribution to the philosophy of the Middle Ages was his rejection, long before Ryle, of the dogma of the ghost in the machine.

His solution is a psychophysical composite, neither of whose components is a complete being: the same kind of composition which is found in every other creature in the physical universe, a composition between a formal and a material principle. But this must not be thought of as a simple combination of "organization" with "elementary particles." It is a metaphysical union of principles of being. This is not an out-moded solution but a grievously misunderstood one. The theory of elementary particles in nowise upsets it. For if there really are elementary particles they will be themselves so composed. And if there are not (Schroedinger, 1950, apparently thought there were not; Dingle has called them "physical symbols," and most physicists think of them apparently as conceptual constructs), they cannot upset the theory of co-principles of being.

It is often contended that modern physics, and especially its applications in cybernetics, has radically altered the problems involved in a philosophy of man. It is worth noting that this has not happened through pronouncements of the greatest physicists but rather through popularized versions. Thus in spite of many disclaimers on the part of all the great physicists, many still believe the billiard-ball analogy of the atom, and many who would reject this in the case of the atom appear to cling to it still in endeavoring to understand the elementary particles. (Cf. Max Born, 1950, and Schroedinger 1950 and 1952.)

The explanatory value of elementary particles is of course beyond question and one can only admire and be grateful to the physicists for their achievements. But in sheer logic it should be pointed out that a concept or set of concepts which "explain" something are not thereby shown to have an ontological counterpart. "Phlogiston" and "ether" are classical examples of concepts which appeared for a time to "explain" phenomena but which were subsequently abandoned for lack of any reality corresponding. Some "explanatory concepts" are "logical fictions." Russell instances geometrical points and instants of time, but there are others. The cycles and epicycles of Ptolemaic astronomy turned out to be logical fictions, and "the unconscious" in contemporary psychology will be seen on reflection to be a good example of an "explanatory concept" which, however convinced one might be of its reality, might turn out to be a logical fiction, for the independent demonstration of its existence turns out to be "impossible by definition."

It is true that most physicists tend to eschew the Schroedinger articles, but then it is also true that most physicists prescind from any discussion of the "real existence" of elementary particles. Their position appears to be expressible in some such form as this: "Something" exists, and these are the explanatory concepts which render it intelligible and (to some extent) controllable. This statement is in no sense intended as a reflection on physics or physicists but only to show that, in spite of *a priori* assumptions to the contrary, the elementary particles do not raise new philosophical problems in the philosophy of man. For it was always clear (except perhaps to pan-psychists) that the organism is material, so that whatever is true of matter will be true of the organism.

The fact that the organism is subject to the law of gravity but that "thought" is not so subject raises the same philosophical problems as are raised by cybernetics or the quantum theory. For the problem is: how can this one individual being, man, or Socrates, whose organism is material (whatever matter is), be also at one and the same time a "thinking thing"? The term "thinking thing" is, of course, Descartes' term but it is used here without prejudice to the theories of Descartes. The watershed which divides all philosophies of man is found right here. For either one assumes that "matter" can think or that it cannot. The fact of thinking is indisputable, but the assumption that matter can think can only be made either by a purely verbal supposition or by ignoring the nature of thinking itself. One could never explain what thinking is to a being who did not already know in some way what thinking is, since the very fact of explanation involves a conscious cognitive receptive being who already knows something, and knows that it knows. It is easy, of course, to make suppositions and to suppose that thought is something other than thought: *e.g.* that is it an electronic process in a complex machine. But all attempts at "reducing" thought to non-cognitive elements will prove unsatisfactory as long as the person who makes the supposition retains conscious awareness, that is, as long as he "knows that he knows." A little reflection will show that this line of speculation will lead to the conclusion that whatever the relation of psychological functions to physiological factors, they are not the same as the physiological factors.

Just as there could be no immortality if there were no soul, so also there could be no immortality if the soul had not already a real existence of its own, or if it were composed of whatever matter is composed of. For the only "immortality" of matter is the tenuous possible "eternity" of its parts, and something which is dependent for its existence on a particular organization of matter or material particles cannot survive the disintegration of such organization. The fact that matter *as such* does not "think," but that man in fact "thinks" is the basis of the argument which establishes the required propositions about soul, *viz.* that it has real existence of its own and that it is not composed of matter.

With regard to the possibility of survival after death, there is an interesting reflection to be made. It is very often asserted in connection with the question *can matter think?* that whereas we know a great deal about what matter can do, any assertion about what it cannot do must be invalid on grounds of apriorism. The assertion that the soul cannot survive the body can be countered by the same reasoning: we know a great deal about soul and what it can do, but any assertion about what it cannot do (*e.g.* that it cannot survive the body) must be invalid on grounds of apriorism. But those who put forward the former argument are not inclined to accept the latter, even though the logic of both is the same; or they are tempted to fall back on simple agnosticism, protesting that they do not know. It is not suggested here that either argument is valid but only that consistency demands the acceptance or rejection of both. The latter does not establish immortality (or even the possibility of it) any more than the former establishes the fact or possibility that matter can think. But it has a special plausibility. The assertion that matter cannot think does not depend simply on what we do not know about matter but rather on what we do know about thought.

The possibility of survival can be established fairly directly. If soul is what we have been contending it is, *viz.* something with an existence of its own and an activity of its own (thought), and is not an organization of matter, it will be seen that it could continue to exist: for these three assertions add up to the notion of immaterial substances. There is no way of establishing this "scientifically" (in Russell's sense of the word). But it is worth recalling that the logic of the thinking involved is the same as that of the scientist who investigates matter. For he infers from the observable (*e.g.* the tracks on a photographic plate) to the unobservable (the inner constitution of matter); just as the philosopher infers from the observable (the behavior of man, including thought) to the unobservable (immaterial substance).

The notion of immaterial substance is foreign both to the scientific mind and the empiricist philosopher. Yet the scientific mind (as witness Sherrington, Adrian, Hinshelwood, Eddington, Einsten and others) finds it easier to accept, even if for the wrong reasons, than does the empiricist philosopher. Compare, for example, Hinshelwood and Ayer. Hinshelwood (1951) appeals to the thomistic theory of angels to illustrate a point about the internal construction of the atom. Ayer (1956) on the other hand finds the notion of spiritual substance unintelligible:

> A view which I have not considered is that people are differentiated from one another . . . by being different spiritual substances or souls. And the reason why I have not considered it is that I do not find it intelligible. (p. 209)

But this statement of his is not really very good philosophizing since "intelligible" has a technical meaning in Ayer (it means something like "capable of withstanding the sort of test which would apply to sensory experience"). And we have already stated that by definition, as it were, this sort of test could not apply. The second reason why Ayer's statement is not very good philosophizing is that to say that one does not find something to be intelligible may very well be a statement about oneself, not about that which is said to be unintelligible.

The question *does this immaterial* (or *"spiritual"*) *substance actually survive the death of the body*? cannot be answered by experiment. And it can be answered in the negative either by a *nego suppositum* argument or by a statement of impossibility. The *nego suppositum* argument would run: "By asking the question you are supposing that there is such a thing as a spiritual substance. But I deny your supposition. Therefore there is no actual survival." The discussion thereupon ceases to be a discussion about immortality and reverts to one about the possibility of there being spiritual substances.

The second form the answer might take is this: "It is impossible that anything should exist apart from matter. Therefore even if there is a spiritual component in man (but in fact, the argument would usually but not necessarily go on, there is not), it could not survive the death of the body." This could very well have been the thinking of the Sadducees or the Greeks with whom St. Paul contended in the Areopagus: "At this mention of rising from the dead some of them burst out laughing" (Ac 17). This argument clearly depends on the assertion that anything should exist apart from matter. But there is no way in which this proposition could be shown to be true. Either it must be assumed dogmatically (which is not good empiricism) or else some proposition which implies it must be assumed. The usual empiricist assumption which is alleged to imply the required proposition is of the form: only what is given in sensory experience exists. This in fact is the essence of empiricism. But neither can it be shown to be true, since there is no sensory test which could possibly be appealed to in order to establish it, and yet a sensory test is the only sort of test allowed in empiricism.

Instead of asking the question in the form *Does the soul survive the body?*, it can be asked in the form: *Does the soul cease to be?* and in this form it becomes much more manageable. For if one can state the ways in which things cease to be and show that these do not apply to the soul, it will follow that it does not cease to be, *i.e.* that it is immortal. It is important to remember, however, that there is an enormous difference between a thing's ceasing to be, on the one hand, and its ceasing to be what it is, on the other. Our only experience of "ceasing to be" is in fact the experience of things ceasing to be what they are. That is to say, we experience change, transformation, resolution into parts, reduction to elements, molecules, atoms or particles. The argument that the soul does not cease to be has a deductive or *a priori* appearance in the form in which it is usually presented, because it is usually presented in a truncated form. In fact it is essentially an inductive piece of reasoning on the basis of experience.

There is one further point: a thing can cease to be red or blue, or hot or cold, or large or small, without ceasing either to be or to be what it is. This kind of ceasing-to-be certainly applies to the soul: it ceases to be conscious or to be actively engaged in thinking or feeling, *etc.* But this is clearly not the kind of ceasing-to-be which is intended in the question of survival, unless one accepts the Humean doctrine which claims that the soul is nothing but a series of such experiences. But this we have already found to be inadequate. On the other hand this kind of ceasing-to-be can help to clear up one difficulty. If the soul were in the same sort of category as "red,", "large" or "hot," if it were a mere quality or quantity or in general an "accident" of the body, then it would be subject to this kind of ceasing-to-be. There were in fact some nineteenth century philosophers who took this line and described *soul* (or more usually *mind*) as an epiphenomenon of the brain. This would still be the point of view, though the terminology might be different, of those who think that electronic brains can "think." But this means in fact, that there is no soul, and if there is no soul there cannot be an immortal soul. Consequently, dealing with this point of view one is not really dealing with immortality but the larger issue of materialism.

There is another obvious fact about accidents: they can cease to be with the destruction of the substance in which they inhere. If the soul were an accident of the body it could cease to be in some such way as this; but then it is not an accident of the body, it is something which has existence and functions of its own. This is clearly not true of the shape of the statue: it has no existence in its own right and there is nothing it can do of itself. One can of course deny the possibility of immaterial (or "spiritual") substance as we have seen, but the assertion: *there are no spiritual substances* is incapable of proof. And the denial itself involves the denial of immortality. Consequently the issue once again is not really the issue of immortality but the antecedent question of the possibility of spiritual substance.

With regard to things other than accidents, the things for instance which are either red or blue or hot or cold, we have already made the assertion that such things do

not cease to be in an absolute sense, but only by becoming'
something else do they cease to be what they are. The difference is enormous. It is the difference between essence and
existence, between infinite and finite causes, between reduction to parts and reduction to nothingness. With regard
to anything which is composed of parts, reduction to its
component parts is possible. If there are not parts such reduction is impossible. The history of the atom illustrates
the point clearly. As long as the atom was regarded as the
"ultimate" constituent of matter it was also regarded as
irreducible. This is why the "splitting of the atom" seemed
to be such an exciting achievement. For the splitting of
the atom meant that it was composed of parts (however
such composition is to be understood) and meant also,
therefore, the abandoning of the supposition that it was
an ultimate particle, with consequential recasting of our
ideas about matter.

The soul is not composed of parts, has no dimensions,
is not quantitative in any way, so that reduction to constituent parts does not arise. The soul has different kinds
of functions and different kinds of capacity for carrying
out such functions, but a capacity (*e.g.* intellect) is not
a component part but an ability to act in a particular way.
This is what is technically called the *simplicity* of the
soul, a term which in English can be misleading. But
simplex as opposed to *complex* carries no such misleading
connotations. *Complex* means composed of parts, but *simplicitas* (from *simplex*) is the quality or property of not
having parts. The *simplicitas* of the soul follows from its
not being composed of whatever matter is composed of,
nor is it a composition of matter and something else. For
the former would mean that it was incapable of thought,
while the latter simply leads to an infinite regress; if there

were such a composition it is the "something else," not the matter in the composition, which would be the soul; and if this something else is so composed then again the soul will be the non-material constituent, and so on.

The conclusion must be that the soul does not cease to be by reduction to parts. And the only alternative remaining for consideration is the possibility of ceasing to be outright; this means annihilation, and the term is used here literally. Does the soul cease to be by its being reduced to nothingness, to non-existence, by an exercise of omnipotent power? Annihilation is the correlative of creation. The latter means causing something to be where there was nothing; the former is the reverse process; and neither is within the compass of finite beings. If God does not annihilate the soul, then it does not cease to be. Does he do so?

There is no doubt that God could, in his omnipotent power, annihilate the soul and one might as well face the fact. But that he does not do so and will not do so follows from our knowledge of God, even such as can be achieved by natural reason without recourse to revelation. For (bearing in mind the difference between finite and infinite and therefore that our terms are to some extent anthropomorphic, or more accurately are used "analogically") it can be shown that God is intellect. He does not therefore act without a purpose. He therefore had a purpose in making the soul the kind of thing it is: a spiritual substance not composed of parts and therefore not subject to the kind of ceasing-to-be to which other creatures are subject. In other words, he made the soul immortal, and he had a purpose in doing so. If now he annihilates the soul, we are faced with a dilemma: either God had no purpose in creating the soul immortal or he now defeats his own purpose. And both consequents are absurd in regard to God. Therefore the soul is not annihilated. Therefore it is immortal.

One must bear in mind the difference between proving a conclusion and winning assent to it. This was Newman's problem in his *"Grammar of Assent."* It is quite clear that people assent to the immortality of the soul for reasons other than those of the above line of argument, and others reject it for reasons other than philosophical ones. But when it is contended that reason cannot establish a proposition or, as with Russell, that it establishes its contradictory, it becomes imperative to try once again to vindicate reason. The problem of immortality is the pivot of metaphysic (Marcel's words) in the sense that one's stand on this problem determines one's stand on all problems of life. Russell in one of his rare emotional passages ("A Free Man's Worship" in *Mysticism and Logic* (1953) falls back on a romantic but perhaps unconvincing Stoicism when he contemplates death.

> One by one, as they march, our comrades vanish from our sight, seized by the silent orders of omnipotent Death. Very brief is the time in which we can help them, in which their happiness or misery is decided. Be it ours to shed sunshine on their path, to lighten their sorrows by the balm of sympathy, to give them the pure joy of a never-tiring affection . . . . Let us remember that they are fellow-sufferers in the same darkness, actors in the same tragedy with ourselves . . . (p. 59).

The notion that life is a tragedy is echoed in existentialist writings: life is absurd and *angoisse* is the key to it. It does not matter what you do, since there are no values, no standards, no criteria, by which to judge the value of life or action. You create your own values in your very strivings for purposes, and whatever purpose you choose gives value to your endeavors to attain it. In the long run, however, you are deceived. The malignant demon of death catches up with you and destroys both your ends and the means you have taken to achieve them. What matters is neither the ends nor the means you have adopted: they are in themselves valueless anyway. What matters is that you should commit yourself wholeheartedly to your ends and means: *engagement total* is the clue (Sartre, 1946). If you are going to be a murderer, be a clever one; a swindler, be a successful one; a traitor, live for treason. The strength of the existentialist movement in philosophy lies in its consistent logic: in its not flinching from drawing the conclusions to which its premises point. Sartre himself described it as an attempt to draw all the conclusions of consistent atheism. But many, like Russell, try to have it both ways: to retain atheism and materialism and at the same time to defend traditional values, even ethical ones. It has often been pointed out that on the materialist hypothesis there can be no values, and Kant went as far as trying to prove the immortality of the soul by a transcendental deduction from the existence of ethical values. At least this much is true: ethical values would be in the long run meaningless without the concept of immortality.

REFERENCES AND RELATED READING

ALLPORT, Gordon: *The Individual and his Religion: A Psychological Interpretation*, New York, Macmillan, 1950.

AYER, A. J.: *Language, Truth and Logic*, 2nd Edition, New York, Dover, 1946.

————: *The Problem of Knowledge*, London, Macmillan, 1956.

————: "The Claims of Philosophy" *in* Natanson, M. (Ed.): *Philosophy of the Social Sciences*, New York, Random House, 1963.

BABIN, Pierre: *Crisis of Faith: The Religious Psychology of Adolescence*, Dublin, Gill, 1964.

BIRMINGHAM & CUNNEEN: *Cross Currents of Psychiatry and Catholic Morality*, New York, Pantheon Books, 1964.

BOUISSON, Maurice: *Magic, its Rites and History*, (Trans. from the French), London, Rider & Co., 1960.

BRACELAND, Francis:' (Ed.) *Faith, Reason and Modern Psychiatry*, New York, Kenedy & Sons, 1955.

BRAIN, Russell: *Science, Philosophy and Religion*, Cambridge University Press, 1959.

BROAD, C. D.: *Lectures on Psychical Research*, London, Routledge & Kegan Paul, 1962.

————: *Perception, Physics and Reality*, Cambridge University Press, 1914.

CAVANAGH, J. & McGOLDRICK, J: *Fundamental Psychiatry*, Cork, Mercier Press, 1963.

Cox, David: *Jung and St. Paul*, London, Longmans Green & Co., 1959.

Farber, S. M., and Wilson, R. H. L., (Eds.,) : *Control of The Mind*, New York, McGraw Hill, 1961.

Fransen, Peter, S.J.: *The New Life of Grace*, (Trans. from the Flemish), London, Chapman, 1969.

Frazer, J.G.: *The Golden Bough*, London, Macmillan, 1922.

Freud, Sigmund: *The Future of an Illusion*, London, Hogarth Press, 1928.

————: *Moses and Monotheism*, (Trans. Katherine Jones). New York, Knopf, 1939.

————: *Civilization and its Discontents*, London, Hogarth Press, 1963.

Fromm, Erich: *Psychoanalysis and Religion*, Yale University Press, 1950.

Gabriel, Fr., ODC: *Visions and Revelations in the Spiritual Life*, Cork, Mercier Press, 1950.

G. A. P. (Group for the Advancement of Psychiatry): *Methods of Forceful Indoctrination*, Symposium No. 4, New York, 1957.

G. A. P. Report: *Mysticism: Spiritual Quest or Psychic Disorder?* Vol. IX, No. 97, New York, 1976.

Gassert, R. G. & Hall, B. H.: *Psychiatry and Religious Faith*, New York, The Viking Press, 1964.

Goldbrunner, Josef: *Individuation: A Study of the Depth Psychology of Jung*, (Trans. from the German), London, Hollis & Carter, 1955.

————: *Holiness is Wholeness*, (Trans. from the German), London, Burns Oates, 1955.

————: *Cure of Mind and Cure of Soul*, (Trans. from the German), London, Burns Oates, 1958.

HADFIELD, J. A.: *"The Influence of Hypnotic Suggestion on Inflammatory Conditions"*, Lancet, 2, pp. 678-679. 1917.

HALEY, Joseph E. (Ed.): *Mental Health and Religious*, Oregon, USA., University of Portland Press, 1965.

HAYNES, Renée: *The Hidden Springs: An Enquiry into Extra-Sensory Perception*, London, Hollis & Carter, 1961.

HERMANN, Ingo: *The Experience of Faith*, New York, Kenedy & Sons, 1966.

HEYWOOD, Rosalind: *The Sixth Sense: An Inquiry into Extra-Sensory Perception*, London, Chatto & Windus, 1959.

HOSTIE, R.: *Religion and the Psychology of Jung*, London, Sheed & Ward, 1957.

HUME, David: *A Treatise of Human Nature*, (First published 1817), Everyman Library Edition, London, Dent, 1911.

HUXLEY, A.: *Control of The Mind*, New York, McGraw Hill, 1961.

INGLIS, Brian: *Fringe Medicine*, London, Faber & Faber, 1964.

JAMES, William: *The Varieties of Religious Experience*, New York, Random House, 1902.

JOHNSON, Paul E: *Psychology of Religion*, New York, Abingdon Press, 1959.

JUNG, C. J.: *Modern Man in Search of a Soul*, London, Routledge & Kegan Paul, 1933.

————: *The Practice of Psychotherapy*, The Collected Works, Vol. 16 (Ed. Sir Herbert Read), London, Routledge, 1954.

KEENAN, Alan: *Neuroses and the Sacraments*, New York, Sheed & Ward, 1950.

KIEV, Ari: *Magic, Faith and Healing*, London, Collier Macmillan, 1964.

KNOX, Ronald: *Enthusiasm*, Oxford University Press, 1950.

LASKI, Marghanita: *Ecstasy: A Study of Some Secular and Religious Experiences*, London, The Cresset Press, 1961

LEON, Philip: *Beyond Belief and Unbelief*, London, Victor Gollancz, 1965.

LIFTON, R. J.: *Thought Reform: A Psychiatric Study of Brainwashing*, London, Gollancz, 1961.

LOUISMET, Dom S: *Mysticism, True and False*, London, Burns Oates & Washbourne, 1924.

MACLEAN, Una: *Magical Medicine*, London, Allen Lane, The Penguin Press, 1971.

MAVES, Paul (Ed): *The Church and Mental Health*, New York, Charles Scribner's Sons, 1953.

MERLAN, Philip: *Brentano and Freud*, Journal of the History of Ideas, Vol. 6, pp. 375-377, 1945

——————: *Brentano and Freud: A Sequel*, Journal of the History of Ideas, Vol. 10, p. 451, 1949.

MERLEAU-PONTY, M: *"The Philosopher and Sociology,"* *in* M. Natanson (Ed.), Philosophy of the Social Sciences, New York, Random House, 1963.

MOORE, G. E.: *Principia Ethica*, Cambridge Univ. Press, 1903.

MOWRER, O. Herbert: *The Crisis in Psychiatry and Religion*, USA., Van Nostrand Co. Inc., 1961.

MYERS, F. W. H.: *Human Personality and its Survival of Body Death*, London, Longmans & Co., 1909.

NATANSON, M. (Ed.): *Philosophy of the Social Sciences*, New York, Random House, 1963.

NEWMAN, J. H.: *A Grammar of Assent*, London, Longmans Green & Co., 1870.

O'DOHERTY, E. F.: *The Priest and Mental Health,* New York, Alba House, 1963.

————: *Religion and Personality Problems,* New York, Alba House, 1964.

————: *Aspects of Man in Religion and Psychology,* (Unpublished papers, Thornfield, University College, Dublin, 1970).

————: *The Psychology of Vocation,* Kent, Faversham Press, 1970.

————: *Consecration and Vows,* Dublin, Gill & Macmillan, 1971.

————: *Vocation and Formation,* Dublin, Gill and Macmillan, 1971.

————: *The Religious Formation of the Elementary School Child,* New York, Alba House, 1973.

OMEZ, REGINALD, Fr.: *Psychical Phenomena,* London, Burns Oates, 1959.

OTTO, Rudolph: *The Idea of the Holy,* (Trans. J. W. Harvey), London, Oxford University Press, 1923.

PRICE, Harry: *The Most Haunted House in England*: *Ten Years' Investigation of Borley Rectory,* London, Harrap, 1940.

————: *The End of Borley Rectory,* London, Harrap, 1946.

RAHNER, Karl: *Studies in Modern Theology,* Freiburg, Herder, and London, Burns Oates, 1965.

RHINE, J. B.: *Extra Sensory Perception,* London, Faber & Faber, 1935.

ROBBINS, Russell: *The Encyclopaedia of Demonology & Witchcraft,* London, Spring Books, 1959.

ROBINSON, John A. T., Bishop of Woolwich: *Honest to God,* London, S.C.M. Press, 1963.

ROSEN, George: *Madness in Society,* London, Routledge & Kegan Paul, 1968.

RUMKE, H. C.: *The Psychology of Unbelief*, (Trans. from the Dutch), London, Rockliff, 1952.

SALMAN, D. H.: *The Psychology of Religious Experience*, Journal of Religion and Mental Health, Vol. 4, No. 5, October, 1965.

SARGANT, William: *Battle for the Mind*: *A Physiology of Conversion and Brainwashing*, London, William Heinemann, 1957.

SIWEK, Paul, SJ: *The Riddle of Konnersreuth*, Dublin, Browne & Nolan, 1954.

SPEARMAN, C: *The Nature of Intelligence and the Principles of Cognition*, London, Macmillan, 1923.

SPINKS, J. S.: *Psychology and Religion*, London, Methuen, 1963.

THOMAS, W. I.: *Social Behavior and Personality*: Contributions of W. I. Thomas to Theory and Social Research, (Ed. Volkart), New York, Soc. Sc. Res. Council, 1951.

THOULESS, Robert H: *An Introduction to the Psychology of Religion*, Cambridge University Press, 1956.

————: *Experimental Psychical Research*, Penguin Books, 1963.

THURSTONE, Herbert: *Ghosts and Poltergeists*, London, Burns & Oates, 1953.

VERGOTE, Antoine: *The Religious Man*, Dublin, Gill & Macmillan, 1969.

WHITE, Victor: *God and the Unconscious*, London, Harvill, 1952.

————: *Soul and Psyche*, London, Collins and Harvill, 1960.

WOODCOCK, George & AVAKUMOVIC, Ian: *The Doukhobors*, London, Faber & Faber, 1968.

WOOTTON, Barbara: *Social Science and Social Pathology*, London, Allen & Unwin, 1959.

ZAEHNER, R. C.: *Mysticism, Sacred and Profane*, England, Clarendon Press, 1957.

————: *Drugs, Mysticism and Makebelieve*, London, Collins, 1972.

ZILBOORG, G.: *Sigmund Freud: His Exploration of the Mind of Man*, New York, Charles Scribner's Sons, 1951.

————: *Freud and Religion*, U.S.A., The Newman Press, 1958.

————: *Psychoanalysis and Religion*, New York, Farrar Strauss & Cudahy, 1962.